Rapid Weight Loss Hypnosis Program For Women: Beginners 21 Day Hypnosis& Affirmations For Fat Burning, Calorie Blast, Mindfulness, Emotional Eating& Cravings (Hypnotic Gastric Band)

By Guided Meditations & Self-Hypnosis Academy

Table of contents:

1 Realistic Big Smart Goal

(30 minutes)

Hello, and welcome to your Rapid Weight Loss Hypnosis Program For Women. Your program is divided into 21 individual hypnotic lessons that will help you on your journey by installing the most useful behaviors, motivation, and thinking patterns for rapid weight loss.

This is your first hypnotic lesson, and it will help you to **create realistic Big SMART goals that will allow you to measure your progress and achieve your desired weight much easier.**

When we say smart goals, what we really mean is that you will be creating goals that are Specific, Measurable, Attainable, Realistic and Timed. When it comes to goal setting this method is proven to work and give great results.

Before you start to think about two or three big goals that you would like to achieve in the next year or two… you can also choose goals that are way beyond just weight loss… imagine goals that come after you already lose weight and have your ideal weight…

Let's begin now…

Find a nice and cozy place where you won't be disturbed… and before you become completely absorbed with the sound of my voice… make yourself comfortable enough to go **into a state of relaxation… you can sit or lie down…** and close your eyes…

This rapid weight loss mindset begins to activate as soon as you intentionally **start to relax and calm yourself down… just like right now** and by realizing… that when **you fill your mind with relaxing thoughts…** any time of the day… **you will feel more energized, motivated and capable of facing any challenge…**

Make final adjustments… and start to focus and follow your breathing… observe mindfully… air going inside and filing your lungs until that point it starts to slowly go out through your nose or mouth…

Make yourself comfortable, and take a deep breath in, to a count of three seconds… one… two… three, hold it for three seconds… two… one… **and let go into relaxation…** take another deep breath through your nose… one… two…three… hold it for three seconds… two… one and **double your relaxation now**… as you gently exhale…

That's right, just like that… **relax** and allow your breathing to happen on its own…

Now, as you are listening to my voice, you can also notice other sounds that are guiding you **into a more relaxed state of mind**… and as you become aware of your relaxation **you can feel relaxation somewhere in your body**… maybe your head… or shoulders… arms or legs… and once you become aware of it… **allow that relaxation feeling to spread and fill your entire body…**

Take a deep breath in, to a count of three seconds… one… two… three, hold it for three seconds… two… one… **and let go into relaxation…**

Take another deep breath through your nose… one… two…three… hold it for three seconds… two… one and **double your relaxation now**… as you gently exhale…
Continue breathing at a steady pace…. just like that... and allow the air moving in and out of your lungs and belly to **deepen your relaxation**...

In a moment I am going to start counting down from five to one... and when you hear me saying "one" **you will completely let go of any remaining tension... negative emotions and thoughts…** spontaneously in your way... **and find yourself going deeper and deeper into relaxation**

Five... **going deeper into relaxation**... four**... letting go of any tension**... three... **letting go of negative emotions**... two... **negative thoughts fading away**... one... **spontaneously In your was... go deeper and deeper into relaxation... that's it just like that...**

Now, In your mind's eye I would like you to imagine a big mental screen in front of you... just like a screen in a movie theatre... and once you have that big mental screen in front of you... imagine a life-size picture of you appears on that screen... step a little bit closer so you can see all the details more clearly... increase the brightness and any colors if needed...

Pay attention to your posture in that picture and ask yourself, **how would you look like if you are regularly setting big goals and following through to achieve desired results?**.... notice how the image of yourself is changing on that screen... **becoming someone who sets big smart goals regularly and following through all the steps until the goals are successfully achieved...**

Be playful and use any idea that comes to your mind... any idea that will make you see yourself making the change you want to be... **improve that picture of yourself on that screen... and as you make small changes.... watch how easily you**

create the best version of yourself.... that sets big goals regularly and follow through to achieve desired results...

Now, as **you see yourself standing there with confidence**... think for a moment where that confidence comes from... and most certainly **you will realize that comes from a great sense of purpose.... having purpose on your mind for each goal gives you that motivation and all necessary energy to achieve your goals...**

Focusing that energy toward your results makes you think in a more strategic way... and to use your time more efficiently than before... you create plans for success, and you stick to your SMART action plans.... see yourself on that screen **confident... with a purpose on your mind... focusing your endless energy toward your big SMART goals** ... where **you set your tasks... schedule activities.... milestones... that you are committed to achieving...**

Everything you do is SMART.... specific outcomes... measurable results.... achievable goals.... relevant to you... timed perfectly... in order for you to **rapidly start losing weight…**

Imagine what you would be thinking and how would you be speaking when you are doing all of this and so much more... in that picture...

Imagine yourself in that picture being absolutely motivated to achieve your weight loss goals and beyond... completely confident in everything you say and everything you do... being unstoppable.... as you are progressing toward achieving all your big smart goals...

Imagine... how would you look like and how would you feel when you achieve all your big SMART goals, and when you are enjoying the fruits of the labor... enjoying the results of your dedicated actions that brought you success with weight loss...

Make that picture... even bigger and brighter.... and once you see it clearly enough.... **imagine stepping into that picture and slowly merge with that image of yourself where you set big smart goals and achieve them regularly**... every year...

Go ahead now step into that picture and slowly in your way become one.... and **as you become one fell that unstoppable confidence... purpose and motivation... all resources**.... look the world around you through your own eyes.... **feeling absolutely motivated to achieve your big smart goals... completely confident in everything you say and everything you do...**

Imagine walking and talking with that kind of confidence and determination to achieve all your

weight loss goals and beyond... by taking SMART actions... planning your success... imagine moving around and notice **how does it feel to be that someone who sets big smart goals regularly and following through all the steps until the goals are successfully achieved...**

Take a deep breath in as **you preserve all the learnings, an internal sense of purpose, and motivation from this guided experience**.... allowing all pieces of information freely flow through your being and connect to each other so **you can become someone who sets big smart goals regularly and following through all the steps until the goals are successfully achieved...**

.... whenever the integration and changes are completed... step out of the screen and slowly head back toward this present moment in time... **bringing all the resources and new mindset that will help you to rapidly start losing weight...**

Allow your other than the conscious mind to observe that wave of integration **filling and connecting your mind and body with the relaxed purpose to rapidly lose weight...** as you slowly start coming back...

In a moment I am going to start counting down from five to one... and when you hear me saying "one" **you will become fully awake, aware and alert...**

Five... **slowly starting to come back**... four... becoming aware of the position of your relaxed body... three... becoming aware of space around you... two... **your big smart goals are clear**... one... open your eyes, and become **fully awake, aware and alert.**

2 Realistic Small Smart Goals

(30 minutes)

Hello, and welcome to your Rapid Weight Loss Hypnosis Program For Women, which will help you on your journey by installing the most useful behaviors, motivation and thinking patterns for rapid weight loss.

This is your second hypnotic lesson and it will help you to **create realistic Small SMART goals, that will allow you to break down your action steps and achieve your desired weight much easier.**

Same as in the first lesson you will be creating goals that are Specific, Measurable, Attainable, Realistic and Timed.

Only this time, instead of thinking about two or three big goals that you would like to achieve in the next year or two… you will choose one of those big goals, and you will break down that goal into smaller smart goals…

Before we start, choose one big smart goal…

Let's begin now…

Find a comfortable place where you won't be disturbed... and before you become completely absorbed with the pleasant sound of this hypnotic lesson... make yourself at ease enough to go **into a state of relaxed mind... you can sit or lie down...** and close your eyes...

This rapid weight loss mindset begins to activate as soon as you intentionally **start to relax and calm your mind and body... just like right now** and by realizing... that when **you consciously choose to relax...** any time of the day... **you will start going into a state of relaxed mind immediately...**

Make final adjustments... and start to focus and follow your breathing... observe with your passive awareness... air going inside and filing your lungs until that point it starts to slowly go out through your nose or mouth...

Make yourself comfortable, and take a deep breath in, to a count of three seconds... one... two... three, hold it for three seconds... two... one... **and let go into relaxation...** take another deep breath through your nose... one... two...three... hold it for three seconds... two... one and **double your relaxation now**... as you gently exhale...

That's right, just like that... **relax** and allow your breathing to happen on its own...

Now, as you listen to my voice, you can also notice other relaxing sounds of this hypnotic lesson... and as you become aware of other relaxing sounds **you can feel relaxation somewhere in your body**... maybe your head... or shoulders... arms or legs... and once you become aware of it... **allow that relaxation feeling to spread and fill your entire body...**

Take a deep breath in, to a count of three seconds... one... two... three, hold it for three seconds... two... one... **and let go into relaxation...**

Take another deep breath through your nose... one... two...three... hold it for three seconds... two... one and **double your relaxation now**... as you gently exhale...
Continue breathing at a steady pace.... just like that... and allow the air moving in and out of your lungs and belly to **deepen your relaxation**...

In a moment I am going to start counting down from five to one... and when you hear me saying "one" **you will completely let go of any distracting thoughts... negativity and stress...** spontaneously in your way... **and find yourself going deeper and deeper into relaxation**

Five... **going deeper into relaxation**... four**... letting go of any distracting thoughts**... three... **letting go**

of negativity... two... **reducing the stress**... one... **spontaneously in your way... go deeper and deeper into relaxation... that's it just like that...**

Now, In your mind's eye I would like you to imagine a big mental screen in front of you... imagine a life-size picture of one of your big smart goals appears on that screen... step a little bit closer so you can see all the details more clearly... increase the brightness and any colors if needed...

You are going to achieve this big goal in one or two years from now... because you are about to make even more detailed actionable steps than before... Imagine that this big goal is actually a movie that is playing over and over again, on that screen, from start to an end or from an end to the start... allowing you to easily spot different chapters of the movie easily...

Each month is one chapter, and each chapter has a beginning and an ending....

So, when you pay attention closely, **you can see what actions you are taking at the beginning of each chapter.... and what results you achieved at the end of each month...**

Each chapter or each month has a specific, measurable, attainable, realistic and timed goal...

Be playful and create mental notes of your actions… **improve the quality of the picture of each chapter on that screen... and as you break down your big goal into easily achievable small smart goals.... notice how your confidence is growing by knowing that you will accomplish your weight loss goals and so much more than that...**

Now, as **you notice that confidence**... think for a moment where that confidence comes from... and most certainly **you will realize that comes from clarity, clear sense of direction and knowing what to do....**

Having clarity, sense of direction and knowing what to do for each monthly goal gives you that certainty in your abilities to achieve your weight loss goals...

Having that certainty in your abilities allows you to use your time more efficiently than before... **you create plans for success, and you stick to your SMART action plans**.... see yourself on that screen **doing what you need to do... set your tasks... schedule activities.... milestones... knowing that you will achieve success...**

Everything you do is SMART.... specific outcomes... measurable results.... achievable monthly goals.... relevant to you... timed perfectly... in order for you to **rapidly start losing weight...**

See yourself in that picture being absolutely certain of your achievements... certain in your ability to lose weight rapidly... completely confident in everything you say and everything you do... being unstoppable.... as you are progressing toward achieving all your small smart goals... each month...

Imagine... how would you look like and how would you feel when you achieve each of your small SMART goals, and when you realize that everything you did is now connecting... and allowing you to accomplish your big smart goals...

Make that picture... even bigger and brighter.... and once you see it clearly enough.... **imagine stepping into that picture and slowly merge with that image of yourself where you set small smart monthly goals and achieve them one by one... each time...**

Go ahead now step into that picture and slowly in your way become one.... and **as you become one fell that unstoppable confidence... clarity and certainty... all resources**.... look the world around you through your own eyes.... **feeling confident that you will achieve all your small smart goals... completely confident in everything you say and everything you do... each month... each day...**

Imagine walking and talking with that kind of confidence and determination to achieve all your weight loss goals and beyond... by taking SMART actions... planning your success... imagine moving around and notice how does it feel to be that someone who sets small smart goals regularly and following through all the steps every day, until the chapter is completed and you move to the next one...

Take a deep breath in as you preserve all the learnings, and internal sense of clarity and certainty from this guided experience.... allowing all pieces of information freely flow through your being and connect to each other so you can become someone who sets small smart monthly goals regularly, and allowing you to accomplish your big smart goals...

.... whenever the integration and changes are completed... step out of the screen and slowly head back toward this present moment in time... bringing all the resources and new mindset that will help you to rapidly start losing weight...

Allow your other than the conscious mind to remember all the action steps for each month, and to fill and connect your mind and body with clarity and certainty on how to rapidly lose weight... as you slowly start coming back...

In a moment I am going to start counting down from five to one... and when you hear me saying "one" **you will become fully awake, aware and alert...**

Five... **slowly starting to come back**... four**...** becoming aware of the position of your relaxed body... three... becoming aware of space around you... two... **your small smart monthly goals are easy**... one... open your eyes, and become **fully awake, aware and alert.**

3 Visualize Your Ideal Outcome

(30 minutes)

Hello, and welcome to your Rapid Weight Loss Hypnosis Program For Women, which will help you on your journey by installing the most useful behaviors, motivation and thinking patterns for rapid weight loss.

This is your third hypnotic lesson and it will help you to **create an attractive vision of your future and desired outcomes, so you can achieve your ideal weight and health goals much easier.**

Now that you have your big and small smart goals set, it is time to energize that actions with a clear vision. To create a vision that will work best for you all you have to do is to think beyond your goals and think about your outcomes. What will you receive and what will you have once you achieve your goals?

In the first two lessons, you had a chance to experience how you would feel once your goal is achieved, and now we will go step further and think about what comes next and what will achieving your goals allow you to have in your life.

Find a comfortable place where you won't be disturbed… and before you become completely absorbed with the pleasant sound of this hypnotic lesson… make yourself at ease enough to go **into a state of relaxed mind... you can sit or lie down...** and close your eyes…

When you **go into a more positive state of mind and release the creative energy of your mind** you can manifest your desired future and feel good about yourself at the end of the day. My voice will guide your mind until you **start naturally creating the future of your dream with the best possible outcomes,** that will help you **have a positive experience and rapidly lose weight…**

This rapid weight loss mindset begins to activate as soon as you intentionally **start to relax and calm your mind and body... just like right now** and by realizing… that when **you consciously choose to relax…** any time of the day… **your creative energy is starting to wake up…**

So as soon as you are ready to **start creating the future of your dream with the best possible outcomes with your creative energy**... simply shift your focus to your breathing… Notice the air going inside your lungs and going out… That's it... now take a deep breath in.... and let it go... gently... **relaxing into a more positive state of mind…**

Breath slowly and deeply… at a pace that is just perfect for you… without effort… **becoming more and more relaxed**… with each breath in… and with each breath out…

In a moment I am going to guide you through breathing techniques, where I will ask you to inhale for four seconds, hold your breath for five seconds and exhale for six seconds. This breathing pattern will help you **become more relaxed** …No effort needed… just follow my voice...

Begin with inhaling slowly to a count of four... three... two... one and hold that breath to a count of five seconds.... four... three... two...one, and slowly exhale to a count of six **as you release all the tension**.... five ...four... three... two... one **completely relaxed now.**

Again, start inhaling to a count of four... three... two... one, hold it for five seconds.... four… three... two... one **and let go into relaxation as you release all remaining tension all the way down... all the way down... That's right... just like that...**

In a moment I am going to start counting from five to one… and when you hear me say "one" **you will completely let go and relax even deeper than before**…

Starting the countdown… five… **going deeper and deeper into a more relaxed state of mind…** four… **gently letting go of distracting thoughts**… three… **going deeper and deep into relaxation**… two… **all the way down… all the way down**… one… **completely relax now… deeper and deeper still… let go… unwind… becoming relaxed more than before…**

Enjoy that relaxation feeling… and notice where relaxation comes from… notice that place in your body that is most relaxed and think of it as a source of your uplifting creative energy…. imagining… that from this source, **rejuvenating and uplifting creative energy spreads in all directions…** reaching all other parts of your body …from head to toes… and from your toes to your head…. **making you have positive and loving thoughts about yourself and others… positive and loving thoughts about the world outside you and inside you…**

Going into a more positive state of mind to naturally release the creative energy of your mind… manifest your desires… and feel good about yourself at the end of the day…

Imagine your favorite color coming out of this source of your uplifting creative energy and spreading in all directions filling every cell of your body…

Feel how **your favorite color makes you think only thoughts you want...** and notice all muscles in your legs... **getting energized**.... your favorite color is filling muscles in your torso.... your chest... your arms and hands... all **filling with this rejuvenating and uplifting creative energy...**

Your entire body is now filled with your favorite color and that rejuvenating uplifting creative energy... from head to toes.... and that color is making **you feel very positive and enthusiastic about all the days ahead of you...**

And I wonder... what is your personal experience of **being completely positive and enthusiastic right now?...**

What is going on inside you right now... that is letting you know... that **you are starting to have more positive end loving thoughts... as you are releasing the creative energy of your mind... and spontaneously begin to create more vivid images of your outcomes... and all the rewards that you will start to receive after each of your big goals is achieved...**

Think about it now... **you achieved your weight loss and health goals... you feel amazing... happy and deeply satisfied...**

Ask yourself... what would all of this give you... what will all of this allow you to have in your life...

something that you didn't have but you wanted to have it… you are finally there and you can have it now…

Allow the perfect vision to unfold in front of you right now as you think about all the outcomes and all the benefits that you will receive once you achieved your goals of rapidly losing weight and being in perfect health…

See yourself experiencing and having all the benefits and rewards form having achieved all your big and small rapid weight loss goals…

See who you become as a person… and how much you have grown after this journey…

Notice what do you believe about life and about yourself as you feel that deep satisfaction of having the outcomes that are even better that you expected…

And as you see and notice all these wonderful changes about you… consider what you can do today **to start being that person right now…** and make sure you have an undeniable experience of **achieving all your small and big goals… and having all the benefits and desired outcomes in the future… now…**

What is the first step that would lead you to create this wonderful change in your life… so you can

feel amazing... happy and deeply satisfied with your accomplishments...

Enjoy this amazing experience... knowing that you can **naturally start creating the future of your dream with best possible outcomes with your creative energy** anytime you want, including now and anytime in the future... and all you have to do is to remember **your favorite color spreading and filling your entire body with rejuvenating uplifting creative energy just like right now...**

Enjoy this moment... and whenever you are ready... slowly... at your own pace... start to come back to this present moment in time....

Allow your other than the conscious mind to remember all the benefits and all the rewards that you will receive , and to **fuel your entire mind and body with all the necessary energy to rapidly lose weight and achieve all your big and small goals easily...** as you slowly start coming back...

In a moment I am going to start counting down from five to one... and when you hear me saying "one" **you will become fully awake, aware and alert...**

Five... **slowly starting to come back...** four... becoming aware of the position of your relaxed body... three... becoming aware of space around you... two... **a clear vision of your desired**

outcomes is in your mind... one... open your eyes, and become **fully awake, aware and alert.**

4 Forget Perfections and Expectations

(30 minutes)

Hello, and welcome to your Rapid Weight Loss Hypnosis Program For Women, which will help you on your journey by installing the most useful behaviors, motivation and thinking patterns for rapid weight loss.

This is your fourth hypnotic lesson and it will help you to **let go of the perfection and huge expectations, avoid feeling overwhelmed, so you can achieve your ideal weight and health goals much easier.**

In your third hypnotic lesson, we built up a perfect and very powerful vision that will fuel you with all the necessary energy to successfully achieve all your small and big goals. Powerful visions of our future outcomes and our future reality can also create strong expectations especially if we took our time to create a perfect and very detailed vision of our future.

In fact, we can set our minds to see only results that we imagined and disregard all other results. For example, we can set our minds to achieve exact weight, and we end up having 3-4 kilograms more. We ignored the fact that muscles are heavier than fat and still trying to achieve our goal even if we already feel that strength, health and energy.

Because your vision is so clear and vivid it might seem like a lot to do right now, while in fact is a series of small steps, one at the time until you reach your destination.

The secret to avoid feeling overwhelmed, and take off any pressure from our actions, is to let go of the form and huge expectations and allow ourselves to focus more on our intentions.

Find a comfortable place where you won't be disturbed… and before you start focusing on my voice and my guidance… make yourself at ease enough to go **into a state of relaxed mind… you can sit or lie down…** and close your eyes…

This rapid weight loss mindset begins to activate as soon as you intentionally **start to relax and calm your mind and body… just like right now** and by realizing… that when **you consciously choose to relax…** any time of the day… **your allow your intention to manifest your goals in many different forms…**

So as soon as you are ready to **start letting go of perfection and overwhelming expectations**... simply shift your focus to your breathing… Notice the air going inside your lungs and going out… That's it... now take a deep breath in.... and let it go... gently... **relaxing into a more peaceful state of mind…**

Breath slowly and deeply… at a pace that is just perfect for you… without effort… **becoming more and more at peace**… with each breath in… and with each breath out…

In a moment I am going to guide you through breathing techniques, where I will ask you to inhale for four seconds, hold your breath for five seconds and exhale for six seconds. This breathing pattern will help you **become more relaxed** ...No effort needed... just follow my voice...

Begin with inhaling slowly to a count of four... three... two... one and hold that breath to a count of five seconds.... four... three... two...one, and slowly exhale to a count of six **as you release all the tension**.... five ...four... three... two... one **completely relaxed now.**

Again, start inhaling to a count of four... three... two... one, hold it for five seconds.... four… three... two... one **and let go into relaxation as you release**

all remaining tension all the way down... all the way down... That's right... just like that...

In a moment I am going to start counting from five to one... and when you hear me say "one" **you will completely let go and relax much deeper than before**...

Starting the countdown... five... **going deeper and deeper into a more peaceful state of mind...** four... **gently letting go of troubling thoughts...** three... **going deeper and deep into relaxation...** two... **all the way down... all the way down...** one... **completely relax now... deeper and deeper still... let go... unwind... becoming peaceful more than before...**

Becoming peaceful allows you to release everyday worries and tension by instructing all small muscles in your feet to **relax**.... and as your feet **begin to relax**... allow that relaxation to slowly move upwards.... up your calves and knees... **making your muscles soft... and lose.... completely relax....** fill that relaxation in your thighs... experiencing that pleasant heaviness of **completely relaxed muscles in your legs...**

Pleasant relaxation is moving up your torso... stomach and lower back.... **becoming even more relaxed...**

And naturally, as relaxation reaches your chest you feel a strong desire to inhale deeply… and fill your lungs with air... as your upper body evenly distributes that relaxation across your shoulders and arm all the way to your fingertips.... and that tingling sensation that you feel in your fingers and palms are there only to remind you that you are about to **go into a peaceful state of mind... perfect for you to completely let go of perfections and overwhelming expectations....** but not just jet... there is no rush...

This will happen on its own... just by **using your strong intention to achieve your weight loss goals**... your body and your subconscious mind will know how to do that for you... once **you are ready to let go... release.... and free yourself completely from achieving imagined perfection...** so that **you can naturally accept achieving your goals and outcomes in many different forms...**

Continue breathing at a steady pace.... just like that... and allow the air moving in and out of your lungs and belly to **deepen your relaxation**...

Imagine that each time you inhale... **relaxation energy fills your head, neck, and chest...** and as you exhale that **relaxation energy spreads through the rest of your body.... just like a wave... filling your head, neck, and chest as you inhale.... and**

spreads that relaxation energy all over your body as it goes down... your arms and bally... all the way down your legs and feet.... **washing away all overwhelming expectations... allowing you to effortlessly move toward your rapid weight loss goals... without pressure... completely at ease... with a strong intention to succeed...**

And each new wave of air brings that relaxation energy... fills your head, neck, and chest... just to simply wash away any narrow focus as you exhale.... **allowing you to see the big picture... effortlessly let go... release... and free yourself completely from the form of your imagination ... naturally... right now... and allow yourself to be surprised with even better results and even better outcomes...**

You don't even have to know if you are ready or not... **to completely let go of everything that was bothering you...** you don't need to anything.... **just allow it to happen naturally on its own.... your body and your subconscious mind know how to let go... surrender to freedom....** as you give yourself permission to **naturally achieve your goals and outcomes in many different forms... with your strong intention...**

And remember that wave of relaxing energy is always there to help you... **let go... release... and**

free yourself completely... each time you inhale... and each time you exhale... **you let go... all perfection and high expectations**.... not only now... and not only here...

Allow your subconscious mind to observe that wave of relaxing energy **filling your mind with acceptance of even better results and outcomes**... Enjoy this moment... and whenever you are ready... slowly... at your own pace... start to come back to this present moment in time.... becoming aware of space around you.... the position of your relaxed body.... all the sound that you hear... including the sound of my voice and the sound of your breath…

Instruct your subconscious mind to remember this mindset and how to be more accepting, so you can recognize your accomplishments and celebrate your achievement **of rapidly losing weight with your strong intention to succeed…**

In a moment I am going to start counting down from five to one... and when you hear me saying "one" **you will become fully awake, aware and alert…**

Five... **slowly starting to come back**... four... becoming aware of the position of your relaxed body... three... becoming aware of space around you... two... **your intention to rapidly lose weight is stronger and stronger**... one... open your eyes, and become **fully awake, aware and alert.**

5 Positive Mindset and Motivation

(30 minutes)

Hello, and welcome to your Rapid Weight Loss Hypnosis Program For Women, that will help you on your journey by installing the most useful behaviors, motivation and thinking patterns for rapid weight loss.

This is your fifth hypnotic lesson and it will help you to **develop a positive mindset and generate an incredible amount of motivation, so you can achieve your ideal weight and health goals much easier.**

In your fourth hypnotic lesson you learned how to avoid feeling overwhelmed, and take off any pressure from your actions, by allow yourselves to focus more on your intentions and to accept achieving your goals in different forms, or in other words, to have different results with same outcomes.

This hypnotic lesson will **elevate your energies and that intention to a higher level.**

So, let's begin…

Find a comfortable place where you won't be disturbed… and before you start concentrating on the tone of my voice… make yourself at ease enough to go **into a state of relaxed mind... you can sit or lie down...** and close your eyes…

This rapid weight loss mindset begins to activate as soon as you intentionally **start to relax and calm your mind and body... just like right now** and by realizing… that when **you consciously choose to relax…** any time of the day… **you can express your true positive nature more easily…**

When you listen to hypnotic lessons like this you are practicing to **passively observe your thoughts, feelings, and sensations in your body.** You also **maintain your focus on what is important and become mindful or develop a relaxed awareness** of your inner world and your surroundings…

Most of the time when we set a goal, there are certain things on our mind that we need to do or expectations that we need to meet… **you might organize our time perfectly,** but do you **remember to organize how are you going to feel and think during your daily activities?**

One of the healthiest things you can do before you start your activities and is to **fill your mind with**

positive thoughts about yourself and about the world around you…

You are here, listening to this program, because you are a loving person… and also, you are here because **you want to have that healthier way of thinking and living**... a way of thinking and living that allows you to be **stress free**... positive thinking that reminds you that **you can accomplish anything you want**… because **your loving nature and intelligence make you unstoppable…**

Make any final adjustments... and start to focus and follow your breathing... **observe mindfully...** air going inside and filing your lungs until that point it starts to slowly go out through your nose or mouth...

Take a deep breath in, to a count of three seconds… one… two… three, hold it for three seconds… two… one… **and let go into relaxation…**

Take another deep breath through your nose… one… two…three… hold it for three seconds… two… one and **double your relaxation now**… as you gently exhale…
Continue breathing at a steady pace.... just like that... and allow the air moving in and out of your lungs and belly to **deepen your relaxation...**

In a moment I am going to start counting from five to one… and when you hear me say "one" **you will completely let go and relax much deeper than before**…

Starting the countdown… five… **going deeper and deeper into a more calming state of mind**… four… **gently letting go of troubling thoughts**… three… **going deeper and deep into relaxation**… two… **all the way down… all the way down**… one… **completely relax now… deeper and deeper still… let go… unwind… becoming relaxed more than before**…

Notice how sounds of this hypnosis lesson creating some **pleasant sensations inside you**…. and as that sound travels through your ears allow that **pleasant sensation of relaxation** start spreading and fill every cell in your head and face.

Feel that tingling sensation of relaxation in every cell… getting stronger and stronger… making you even more relaxed… as you double the comfort you are experiencing right now…

And because all your cells are connected… and share the same experience of **comfort…. and relaxation…** that means… all other cells in your body can **relax right now…**

That pleasant sensation of tranquility and peace... is sending the signal to all the cells in your body... **relax.... connect with yourself.... connect to your true positive nature...** starting from your head and face... notice how this signal travels down your neck.... **filing every cell with relaxation....** down your shoulders and arms.... **pleasant tingling sensation of comfort.....** your chest.... back... and stomach... **know how to relax....** just by observing and allowing the signal of relaxation to keep spreading down your legs and feet and all the way back to your head.... creating that **continuous cycle of tranquility and peace inside your body right now... turning on your positive nature...**

If pleasant sounds that you hear can make **you feel more relaxed....** in the same way **positive thoughts can make you feel more energized and motivated** to accomplish anything you like... including your goal to **rapidly lose weight...**

And as your breath follow this **continuous cycle of tranquility and peace in your body...** that elevates your positive nature... you can notice that you have more and more positive **thoughts... and the more positive thoughts you have, the more energized and motivated you to feel... the more energized and motivated you to feel the more your intention becomes stronger... and the more your intention**

becomes stronger more easier it becomes for you to achieve your rapid weight loss goals...

Imagine being in a safe space... it can be indoors or outdoors... familiar or imagined place... in any case, **you feel very safe being at this place and you feel very relaxed**... perhaps you can find a nice and cozy spot in this safe place where you can sit and **make yourself comfortable for a moment...**

And as you sit... notice **how your relaxation deepens**... and **your positivity and motivation grow bigger inside you... convincing you that you can overcome any challenge and achieve your weight loss goals...**

As you are feeling your positivity and motivation getting stronger and stronger... suddenly you see a small paper scroll next to you... kind of scroll that is used for important messages...

Naturally, you reach out and take the paper scroll in your hand and open it... only to see **the most powerful affirmations inside**... affirmations that will **increase your positivity and motivation... elevate your energies and intentions... and make you achieve your rapid weight loss goals more easily...**

Read these affirmations, repeat them inside your mind... and each time you read and repeat any affirmation… imagine that you are saying it louder and louder…

From this moment forward I invite unlimited positivity and motivation into my life!

Repeat it much louder inside your mind…

I am an unlimited and unstoppable source of energy and powerful intention… I can do anything!

Repeat it louder and hear this affirmation echoing into distance everywhere around you…

I am grateful for all the beauty that I have in my life, inside and out!

Turn the volume up… let your voice reach all corners of the Earth…

In every challenge I see the opportunity to grow and achieve my goals!

Repeated even louder than before…

One more affirmation…

I attract the best circumstances and people in my life with my positive mindset... I have everything I need to achieve my rapid weight loss goals!

Repeat it in your mind so loudly that the whole universe can hear you...

As soon as you repeat these affirmations **notice how much more energy and motivation you have...**

Focus this power on creating solutions... overcoming challenges and achieving your weight and health goals...

Passively observe with your relaxed awareness that energy and motivation are **filling your mind and body and clearing the road ahead of you...** as you slowly start coming back...

In a moment I am going to start counting down from five to one... and when you hear me saying "one" **you will become fully awake, aware and alert, feeling energized and motivated to start rapidly losing weight today...**

Five... **slowly starting to come back...** four... becoming aware of the position of your relaxed body... three... becoming aware of space around you... two... **your energy and motivation are growing stronger...** one... open your eyes, stretch your body as you become **fully awake, aware and alert... feeling energized and motivated to start rapidly losing weight today.**

6 Develop Consistency

(30 minutes)

Hello, and welcome to your Rapid Weight Loss Hypnosis Program For Women, that will help you on your journey by installing the most useful behaviors, motivation and thinking patterns for rapid weight loss.

This is your sixth hypnotic lesson and it will help you to **become more consistent when pursuing the life you want, so you can achieve your ideal weight and health goals much easier.**

In your fifth hypnotic lesson you learned how to elevate your energies and intention to achieve your rapid weight loss goals by filling your mind with positive thoughts about your self and the world around you.

You will be using this elevated energy and intention to become consistent in your efforts to fulfill your plans and enjoy a healthier lifestyle more fully.

So, let's begin…

Find a comfortable place where you won't be disturbed… and before you start concentrating on the tone of my voice… make yourself at ease enough to go **into a state of relaxed mind... you can sit or lie down...** and close your eyes…

This rapid weight loss mindset begins to activate as soon as you intentionally **start to relax and calm your mind and body... just like right now** and by realizing… that when **you consciously choose to relax…** any time of the day… **you can express your true positive nature more easily…**

Make any final adjustments... and start to focus and follow your breathing... **observe mindfully...** air going inside and filing your lungs until that point it starts to slowly go out through your nose or mouth... and pay attention to that point where breathing in stops and breathing out begins… a pure moment of silence and stillness of your mind and body…

Mindfully follow the air going in and out through your nose.... slowly inhale.... and exhale.... air going in..... and air going out... **relaxing**… and notice... mindfully... the slight difference in temperature of that air as you let it go out.... going deeper as you focus on the tiny area between your upper lip and your nostrils.... and notice all sensations of air going in..... and air going out... and the slight difference in the temperature of that air... **relaxing** each time you inhale... and **relaxing** even deeper every time you exhale....

Observe your breathing mindfully and as you do that notice all the sensations and the way your body makes subtle calm movements… and if it happens that your attention wanders… from one thought to another… just bring your focus back on your breathing and **continue to deepen your relaxation…**

Focus on the air flowing through your nose... and feel your breath going down your through into your lungs… your chest or belly rises… then the moment of stillness between breaths… and then air flowing out your mouth**… feeling so relaxed right now…**

Make your breath even by making you inhalation and exhalation the same… inhale for five seconds and exhale for five seconds… count inside your mind…

Inhaling… one… two… three… four… five… relaxing

Exhaling… one… two… three… four… five… relaxing

Inhaling… one… two… three… four… five… relaxing

Exhaling… one… two… three… four… five… relaxing

That's right you are doing great…. **feeling very relaxed now…**

In a moment I am going to start counting from ten to one… and when you hear me say "one" **you will completely let go and double your relaxation**

Starting the countdown… five… **going deeper and deeper into relaxation…** four… **gently letting go and allowing thoughts to pass by**… three… **going deeper and deep into relaxation**… two… **all the way down… all the way down**… one… **completely relax now… deeper and deeper still… double your relaxation…**

Now that your more mindful of this moment… shift your focus to your body and notice the position of your body at this moment…. follow any signals and suggestion from your subconscious mind to **make yourself more comfortable**… perhaps you need to adjust the positions of your arms and hands and make them rest on the side of your body… or in any way **that feels most comfortable for you**….

And as you continue to breathe in a normal steady pace… I would like you to imagine your perfect calm and safe place…. a place where you can observe all your actions… and evaluate your own performance and efficiency…

Imagine that in this space there is a comfortable chair with behind a work desk.... go ahead and sit in that comfortable chair behind that work desk...

In this calm and safe place, **you can make sure you are using your time wisely...** and recent changes in your life.... decision to **rapidly lose weight and achieve your health goals** require you to make some additional rules…

You recognize the need to **turn on your will power and become consistent in taking actions and progressing toward your rapid weight loss goals**… **so you can make sure you enjoy all the benefits and all blessings that will come with your new healthy lifestyle…**

The first thing that you do is that you **decide how much time you want to dedicate each day to work on your weight and health goals…** Think of all the meals you plan to have… all the exercises you want to do… all the activities and all the actions… and all the habits you want to develop that are connected to your healthy lifestyle… allow images of those exercises activities, actions and habits to appear in front of you…

On the table you can see a calendar for the whole year… you make an entry and you schedule all activities, actions and habits for each day of the year… that you are going to take in order to **achieve your rapid weight loss goals… making sure that they fit your healthy lifestyle…**

Every time you see the reminder to do some activity, take action or install a habit you will **feel great will power and your desire to be consistent** because you know it will pay off and you will achieve success…

So, as you are sitting in that comfortable chair behind that work desk, in this calm and safe place… **designed for you to make sure that you are using your time wisely and efficiently**… you decide to hire a personal assistant… consistency and will power manager… that will **constantly remind you of all the activities, actions and habits you need to be doing to accomplish your rapid weight loss goals…**

Choose any assistant you like that will be perfect for this function and suitable for your personal needs… someone who knows how to remind you in the right moment so you **instantly start feeling increased will power and desire to be consistent with your healthy life choices…**

As they arrive, greet them and thank them for coming to assist you on your way to **successfully accomplish your weight and health goals...** show them your yearly calendar with all the scheduled activities and explain their role... and how would you like things to be done... and that includes making any changes to your schedule so you can **enjoy your healthy lifestyle even more...**

Your assistant wishes to make a deeper connection with you and to show you they will be devoted to this assignment.... So, they create a ball of consistency energy that contains **unlimited will power**... you slowly reach out and take the ball of consistency energy with your hands... and gently...slowly bring it closer to your chest...

Allow that ball of energy filled with the will power to enter your body and **feel that consistency energy growing bigger and stronger inside you... and integrate it with you being...**

Confirm the integration of your consistency energy by inhaling now deeply and slowly... hold your breath for three seconds... two... one... and exhale slowly... as **you allow will power flow through your body easily and effortlessly**... charging every activity, action and habit...

Passively observe with your relaxed awareness that **consistency energy filling your mind and body with willpower...** as you slowly start coming back...

In a moment I am going to start counting down from five to one... and when you hear me saying "one" **you will become fully awake, aware and alert...**

Five... **slowly starting to come back...** four... becoming aware of the position of your relaxed body... three... becoming aware of space around you... two... **your consistency energy is growing stronger...** one... open your eyes, stretch your body as you become **fully awake, aware and alert.**

7 Enjoy the Journey and Make It Fun

(30 minutes)

Hello, and welcome to your Rapid Weight Loss Hypnosis Program For Women, which will help you on your journey by installing the most useful behaviors, motivation and thinking patterns for rapid weight loss.

This is your seventh hypnotic lesson and it will help you to **develop a playful personality to make this journey more enjoyable and more fun, so you can achieve your ideal weight and health goals much easier.**

In your sixth hypnotic lesson you learned how to install unlimited will power and consistency when doing activities, taking actions and creating new habits that will lead you to your rapid weight loss goal.

This hypnotic lesson makes your consistency even more attractive by adding playfulness and by choosing an attitude to have fun in everything that you do.

When we say playfulness, we still mean being devoted to your weight loss goals and doing whatever is necessary to achieve those goals in a healthy way. That includes not being too serious and working without unnecessary pressure or stress.

So, let's begin…

Find a comfortable place where you won't be disturbed… and before you start concentrating on the tone of my voice… make yourself at ease enough to go **into a state of relaxed mind… you can sit or lie down…** and close your eyes…

This rapid weight loss mindset begins to activate as soon as you intentionally **start to relax and calm your mind and body… just like right now** and by realizing… that when **you consciously choose to relax…** any time of the day… **you can become more playful and make your journey enjoyable and fun…**

Start **instructing your body and mind to relax**… notice how you breathe. And as you start to focus and follow your breathing... I would like you to carefully listen to all the sounds you can hear right now... including the sound of your breathing…

Inhale slowly… hold it for a one second…. and let go... listen to all the sounds you hear including the sound you make as you inhale... and as you exhale…

and notice how every time you exhale like this, with your attention on all the sounds you hear, **you instantly start feeling more relaxed... you start feeling more at ease...**

Calmly listen to all the sound, including the sound of your breath, with your awareness and observe mindfully... sounds you make as you inhale... and as exhale... **feeling so relaxed right now...**

Decide to double your relaxation next time air start going out by exhaling slower than usual and listen to that sound of exhalation until you **completely let go of all distracting thoughts....** reminding yourself that this is your time.... and that you are here because **you want to align your consistency in taking action with playfulness...**

In a moment, I am going to start counting from ten to one... and when you hear me say "one" **you will completely let go and double your relaxation**

Starting the countdown... five... **going deeper and deeper into relaxation...** four... **gently letting go and allowing thoughts to pass by...** three... **going deeper and deep into relaxation...** two... **all the way down... all the way down...** one... **completely relax now... deeper and deeper still... double your relaxation...**

As you feel this deep relaxation starts focusing on becoming more playful… and becoming playful is easy because everyone has playfulness inside… it is your inherited trait and it comes naturally to you… and that means you can experience fun and joy naturally anytime you choose to do so…

Being playful when pursuing your goals allows you to **meet challenges with humor and lightheartedness…** and that takes off all unnecessary stress… giving you the opportunity to **enjoy the journey… go with the flow… and have fun as you rapidly lose weight…**

To **completely aligned your consistency energy with playfulness**… I would like you to imagine that there is a brilliant light above your head...

Feel the presence of that brilliant light above the top of your head.... and allow that brilliant light to fill up your entire body... starting with your head... imagine every cell in your head filled with that brilliant light... **waking up your inner child and playfulness within you…**

This brilliant light is now felling your neck... gently flowing toward your shoulders... filling every inch of your arms... all the way to your fingertips... **feeling joyfulness and happiness growing bigger inside you…**

Notice how your back, chest and stomach muscles **become rejuvenated and refreshed as soon as you see and feel that brilliant light filling your upper body**...

Continue to **align your consistency in taking action with playfulness...** and follow that brilliant light with your awareness as it goes down toward your legs...

Find a perfect balance between being working and being playful... and realize you can have the best of both of these worlds... focus on your **determination to successfully accomplish your rapid weight loss goals** and think about the time when you were very playful... think about all those pleasant happy memories of you being playful and notice how everything that you wanted to do seamed much easier...

Step in that pleasant happy memory and feel once again what it was like to be that playful... how was it to have fun.... Notice how did you feel and what did you do to be playful...

Recognize that inner child inside you and **reconnect with all the fun and joy that you can experience while pursuing your rapid weight loss goals...**

That inner child is always present inside you and waiting for your permission to **start playing and fully express that inherited trait to enjoy life and enjoy the journey… as you rapidly lose weight as you have fun…**

Think about all the things you are planning to do today or tomorrow… think about places that you will go and the activities that you will be doing…

Make distinctions between actions that require you to be only playful or actions that require you to be serious to a certain point… and notice the difference…

Imagine that everything you do, you are either **being completely playful, or you have that perfectly balanced playful personality that allows you to be serious enough and have fun at the same time…** imagine now what this would be like…

See yourself… **being completely playful as you are doing some activities on your own… and see yourself playfully get the job done…**

And as you think about yourself **being and becoming more playful…** hear me saying this affirmations and repeat them inside your mind and attach them to your plans and activities that you will be doing today or tomorrow or any other day…

It's ok to have a playful personality.

I allow myself to be playful.

I can be serious when needed, and playful at times.

I behave in a playful way when I meet challenges.

I am playful when pursuing my goals.

I love my life and I completely enjoy it at this moment.

I let myself be playful every day.

I find joy in what I do and who I am as a person.

I take action towards my goals and have fun while doing so.

I create unlimited playful energy for myself.

Go ahead now and attach each of these affirmations to your plans and activities that you will be doing today or tomorrow or any other day… and notice how this makes you feel…

Passively observe with your relaxed awareness that playfulness **filling your mind and body and notice how light you feel**... knowing that **you can achieve your weight and health goals much easier, enjoy the journey and have fun while doing so...**

In a moment I am going to start counting down from five to one... and when you hear me saying "one" **you will become fully awake, aware and alert... ready to accept your inner child and give yourself permission to be more playful while achieving your weight loss and health goals...**

Five... **slowly starting to come back...** four... becoming aware of the position of your relaxed body... three... becoming aware of space around you... two... **your energy and motivation are growing stronger...** one... open your eyes, stretch your body as you become **fully awake, aware and alert... ready to accept your inner child and give yourself permission to be more playful while achieving your weight loss and health goals.**

8 Morning Routine

(30 minutes)

Hello, and welcome to your Rapid Weight Loss Hypnosis Program For Women, which will help you on your journey by installing the most useful behaviors, motivation and thinking patterns for rapid weight loss.

This is your eight hypnotic lesson. It will help you **create a powerful morning routine that you can repeat every day, so you can achieve your ideal weight and health goals much easier.**

In your seventh hypnotic lesson you learned how to **pursue your rapid weight loss goals by being playful and enjoying the process of change**, without pressure or stress.

This hypnotic lesson will suggest the most successful morning routine for that you can use to **playfully start your day and develop a habit of a healthier lifestyle**, that will ultimately lead you to **achieve your weight and health goals**.

So, let's begin…

Find a comfortable place where you won't be disturbed… and before you start concentrating on the tone of my voice… make yourself at ease enough to go **into a state of relaxed mind... you can sit or lie down...** and close your eyes…

This rapid weight loss mindset begins to activate as soon as you intentionally **start to relax and calm your mind and body... just like right now** and by realizing… that when **you consciously choose to relax...** any time of the day… **you can set your self up for success and achieve even more than you think…**

Start **instructing your body and mind to relax**... notice how you breathe. And as you start to focus and follow your breathing... I would like you to carefully listen to the sound of my voice that you can hear right now... including the sound of your breathing…

Inhale slowly… hold it for a one second.... and let go... listen to all the sounds you hear including the sound you make as you inhale... and as you exhale… and notice how every time you exhale like this, with your attention resting on the sound of my voice, **you instantly start feeling more relaxed... you start feeling more at ease... allowing yourself to become calm...**

Calmly listen to all the sound, including the sound of your breath, with your awareness and observe mindfully... sounds you make as you inhale… and as you exhale... **feeling so relaxed right now…**

Decide to double your relaxation next time air start going out by exhaling slower than usual… make your exhalation longer… and listen to that sound of exhalation until you **completely let go of all thoughts**.... reminding yourself that this is your time.... and that you are here because **you want to develop a morning routine that will build your character and achieve all your rapid weight loss and health goals…**

You can allow yourself to completely empty your mind from all the thoughts right now… by becoming aware of your passive awareness… **thoughts are passing by like clouds in the sky… passively being aware of everything inside you… knowing that passively observing your inner world can only bring you calmness and peace…**

In a moment I am going to start counting from five to one… and when you hear me say "one" **you will completely let go and double your relaxation…**

Starting the countdown now… five… **going deeper and deeper into relaxation…** four… **gently letting go and allowing thoughts to pass by**… three… **going deeper and deep into relaxation**… two… **all**

the way down... all the way down... one... **completely relax now... deeper and deeper still... double your relaxation...**

Now that **you are experiencing a deep level of relaxation and awareness**... allow yourself to think of the nearest door to you...

Out there you might know where this door will lead you... but inside your mind... this door can lead you to many different places... and one of those places is a perfect bedroom...

Go ahead now imagine walking toward that door... grab the doorknob and turn it... open the door and enter the perfect bedroom...

Once inside, notice a big and most inviting bad you could imagine... lie down on this bad so **you can go into an even deeper state of relaxation...**

In front of you, in the center of the room, there is a big tv screen... and on the screen, you can see seven tasks that create a powerful morning routine that **you can use to create habits for your rapid weight loss program...**

The first task- Drink warm lemon water.

The second task - Get some sun and go for a walk.

Third task - Cold shower

Fourth task - High-Protein Breakfast

Fifth task - Practice mindfulness and meditation

The sixth task - Set your intentions for the day.

The seventh task - Prepare your diet plan for the day

Movie begins and you watch yourself on that screen doing your powerful morning routine… you see yourself doing each task in a relaxed manner and having fun by doing so…

On the screen you see that the moment you wake up you stretch, and you think to yourself that **this is going to be a great day…**

You get out of the bed and once you are ready you go to your kitchen and **have a glass or two of warm lemon flavored water**… knowing that this task is **helping you detox, improve your immune system and speed up your metabolism so you can start losing weight much quicker…**

After you watched hydrating yourself, next you see yourself **going out for fresh air, to catch some sun and go for a power walk… knowing that this task will increase your energies and burn fat faster than before…**

This morning walk **wakes up your entire system… gets rid off old unused energies and fill your body** and mind with more useful energies for weight loss…

When you come back from your power walk you **see yourself taking a cold shower… you wash away any remaining negativity… and improved circulation boosts your immune system and makes you become more focused and alert…** cold shower washes away all toxins that you got reed of through sweating… and you notice how much lighter you feel…

After refreshing yourself with a nice cold shower you **see yourself enjoying a high-protein breakfast… that regulates your appetite, feeds your muscles and burns more calories… making your weight loss more permanent… and giving you that extra mental performance improvement…** See yourself on that screen rapidly losing weight for sticking to this task…

Once that task is completed you move on to the next task and that is **your practice of mindfulness and meditation…** See yourself on that tv screen, **practicing mindful meditation…** doing all kinds of breathwork and… **observing with relaxed awareness and compassion the world inside you and around you…**

Mindfulness and meditation practice naturality bring you to your next task in your powerful morning routine…

Since **you are already relaxed, your mind is clear and in touch with your inner world** it is time to see yourself setting your intentions for that day… starting with the first step of preparing your diet for the whole day…

Decide right now how are you going to feel during your day… **what positive emotions are you going to experience**… how will you behave and react to different situations… how will you meet any challenges if they occur…

See yourself on that screen setting clear intentions for that day and **accomplishing everything you wanted to do that day… feeling deeply satisfied at the end of the perfect day…**

The movie continues and you watch yourself doing the first step, preparing your diet plan for that day, after setting your intentions… see yourself preparing all your healthy meals, snacks and nutrition drinks that are part of your rapid weight loss diet… notice how **you enjoy having well planned healthy food throughout the day…**

As the movie comes to an end you imagine that tv screen are becoming smaller and smaller… and once its is small enough, imagine taking that tv screen, that is playing powerful morning routine over and over again and gently place it inside your mind as a symbol of your desire to **build your character with these habits and achieve all your rapid weight loss and health goals… do this now install powerful morning routine into your inner being…**

In a moment I am going to start counting down from five to one… and when you hear me saying "one" **you will become fully awake, aware and alert… and find yourself doing this morning routine spontaneously…**

Five… **slowly starting to come back**… four… becoming aware of the position of your relaxed body… three… becoming aware of space around you… two… **your energy and motivation are growing stronger**… one… open your eyes, stretch your body as you become **fully awake, aware and alert… and find yourself doing this morning routine spontaneously.**

9 Mindfulness and Meditation

(30 minutes)

Hello, and welcome to your Rapid Weight Loss Hypnosis Program For Women, that will help you on your journey by installing the most useful behaviors, motivation and thinking patterns for rapid weight loss.

This is your ninth hypnotic lesson and it will help you to have a better mindfulness meditation practice, **so you can achieve your ideal weight and health goals much easier.**

In your eighth hypnotic lesson you learned how to install a powerful morning routine to continuously progress toward your weight and health goals. Remember that sticking to your morning routine with your will power and strong intention to succeed, will build up your character to achieve rapid weight loss goals and even more than that.

When you meditate you are practicing to **passively observe your thoughts, feelings, and sensations in your body**. Guided meditations can help you develop a routine that you can follow on your own once you feel comfortable to **maintain your focus and become mindful, or develop a relaxed awareness** of your inner world and your surroundings.

You can do meditation anytime of the day, however you should know that the best time to practice meditation is when you wake up or just before you go to sleep.

So, let's begin…

This guided meditation that is specially designed to help you **go into a deep blissful relaxation**…. my voice will assist you and guide your mind and your body until **you feel completely relaxed and at ease in just a few minutes**… so just find a comfortable place where you won't be disturbed… and before you start concentrating on the tone of my voice… make yourself at ease enough to go **into a state of relaxed mind… you can sit or lie down…** and close your eyes…

This rapid weight loss mindset begins to activate as soon as you intentionally **start to relax and calm your mind and body… just like right now** and by realizing… that when **you consciously choose to relax…** any time of the day… **you can start having a deeply relaxing mindful meditation practice…**

So as soon as you are ready to **start going into a more relaxed state of mind and body**... simply shift your focus to your breathing. Notice the air going inside your lungs and going out. That's it... now take a deep breath in.... and let it go... gently.... **relaxing**...

And **to continue relaxing even more**.... take another slow and deep breath in now.... and gently.... let it go... all the way out... **as you feel getting more relaxed**.

And as **you feel getting more relaxed** allow your breathing to naturally happen on its own... collect all the tension when you inhale... and let it all go... **and relax... every time you exhale... deepening your relaxation** every time… and not only like that, but also any way that is most natural to you to **relax now**.... as you listen to my voice and pleasant sounds of this guided meditation...

Enjoy that relaxation feeling as you think about the position of your body right now.... notice what kind of final adjustment can you make to **increase your comfort... and double your relaxation**.... as soon as you make all the adjustments.... **make yourself comfortable... and prepare yourself, go even deeper into relaxation... right now…**

All adjustments being made now allow you to scan your entire body more easily... from head to toes…

and from your toes to your head… and as you scan your body with your awareness... just like that... I want you to **notice all your muscles starting to relax...** notice all muscles in your feet... **getting relaxed....** muscles in your calves... **getting relaxed...** muscles in your thighs... **your lower body is now completely relaxed...**

Instruct all the muscles in your torso to **relaxed**... your chest muscles... **relax....** your arms and hands... **relax...** your back... **relax...** your neck... **relax...**your head... **relax....**

Relaxation spreads across your face… muscles on your chin…. mouth... chicks… nose... and all the tiny muscles around your eyes…. and forehead... all getting very…. **very relaxed now**...

Your entire body is now deeply relaxed and all that is left for you to do is to become aware of your thoughts in your mind right now...

Being aware of your thoughts and **passively observing the process of thinking** is the secret to good mindfulness and meditation practice… allowing your thoughts to appear on your big mental screen in the center of your awareness…

Focus on **just being a passive observer**, practically ignoring your thoughts but being aware of them at the same time… **observe them calmly** without the desire to get involved with your thoughts or act upon your thoughts in any way**… just be present in this moment**….

Be completely still and mindful… Noticing how the mind is trying to invite you to get involved in the content of the thoughts and create a story… **stay calm and keep observing without wanting to change anything** or to interact with any of your thoughts**… let them go**… **you are only a witness of your thoughts** that are passing by just like clouds in the sky… coming and going… thoughts fading away…

And if you do find yourself interacting with a thought or that your mind starts to wonder… the moment you realize this simply **shift your focus back to your breathing and you will become mindful again… and bring yourself back to this present moment… right here and right now… aware of your body… aware of any sound you hear…** including the sounds of my voice and the relaxing sound of your breathing…

Beside thoughts, you may become conscious of different emotions that can spontaneously arise within you while you practice meditation...

Similarly, just like you were observing your thoughts with your passive awareness… in the same way, start observing your emotions… allowing them to be there…

Whatever emotion appears inside your body or mind welcome it… become aware of it **without a desire to act upon it… just let it be there…** present together with you at this moment…

Depending on which emotion is being present in your body or mind, you might catch yourself having a desire to hold on to it and dive into positive emotions… or you can find yourself wanting to run away or dismiss negative emotions…

Remember to be completely still and mindful… stay calm and keep observing without wanting to change anything or to interact with any of your emotions… positive or negative… **let them go… you are only a witness of your present emotions** that are passing by just like clouds in the sky… coming and going…

At this point, **you are experiencing a great sense of mindful relaxation**…. and I wonder… what is your personal experience of **being completely mindful right now**….

Anyway, you are experiencing deep mindful relaxation of your mind and body is just perfect… and you can allow yourself to **completely surrender… and let go…**

Completely... and enjoy this amazing relaxing and mindful experience... knowing that **you can have good mindful meditation practice anytime you want**, including now and anytime in the future... and all you have to do is **shift your focus back to your breathing and you will become mindful again**... instantly relaxed... **present at this moment... right here and right now... in a perfect mindset to achieve your rapid weight loss goals...**

Enjoy this deeply relaxing moment.... enjoy being mindful… and whenever you are ready... slowly… at your own pace... become aware of your surroundings.... come back to this room....

Passively observe with your relaxed mindful awareness expanded consciousness **filling your mind and body**... as you slowly start coming back...

In a moment I am going to start counting down from five to one... and when you hear me saying "one" **you will become fully awake, aware and alert, feeling calm, relaxed and confident in your ability to have great mindfulness meditation practice...**

Five... **slowly starting to come back**... four... becoming aware of the position of your relaxed body... three... becoming aware of space around you... two... **your mindfulness of the present moment becoming stronger**... one... open your eyes, stretch your body as you become **fully awake,** aware and alert... feeling calm, relaxed and confident in your ability to have great mindfulness meditation practice as a part of your powerful morning routine, so you can easily achieve your weight and health goals.

10 Calorie Reduction

(30 minutes)

Hello, and welcome to your Rapid Weight Loss Hypnosis Program For Women, which will help you on your journey by installing the most useful behaviors, motivation, and thinking patterns for rapid weight loss.

This is your tenth hypnotic lesson and it will help you to **reduce your calories by becoming more mindful while you are eating and deciding on the size of your meal portions, so you can achieve your ideal weight and health goals much easier.**

In your ninth hypnotic lesson, you learned how to meditate and become more mindful of this present moment and to be aware of your physical body, your thoughts and your emotions without judgment. Being in the now and being mindful is a very desirable and beneficial state of mind to make good decisions that are aligned with your goals and based on your higher values.

This hypnotic lesson you will extend your mindfulness from your meditation practice into your normal waking life, **so you can effortlessly achieve your rapid weight loss goals.**

So, let's begin…

Find a comfortable place where you won't be disturbed… and before you start following the sound of my voice into relaxation… make yourself at ease, enough to increase your comfort**... you can sit or lie down...** and close your eyes…

This rapid weight loss mindset begins to activate as soon as you intentionally **start to relax and calm your mind and body... just like right now** and by realizing… that when **you consciously choose to relax…** any time of the day… **you can express your true positive nature more easily…**

Begin your mindfulness practice by taking a few long, slow, deep breaths… inhaling deeply… and exhaling very slowly…. inhale through your nose or mouth and exhale through your nose or mouth… **becoming relaxed**… Feel your belly expand when you breathe in and **relax and let go** as you breathe out…

Become aware of all internal and external sounds… and begin to shift your focus from outside sensations to your internal experience of your inner world… and **sense relaxation starting to fill your body and mind**… If you are interrupted by any distracting sound, acknowledge it and bring back your attention back to your breathing and pleasant sounds of this hypnotic lesson.... and continue to **observe relaxation feelings...**

Now we are going to do a progressive body relaxation and we will start from your feet...

Become aware of the sensations in your feet... move your toes briefly and **allow relaxation to be present** in your feet and toes....

Feel your feet **filled with relaxation**... and use your will power to move that relaxation up to your ankles... calves... knees and thighs... all **getting filled with relaxation**... mindfully be aware of the **deep relaxing sensations in your legs**...

If you find your mind wandering as **you deepen your relaxation**... acknowledge that too for a moment... and without judgment bring your focus back to your breathing and continue your journey by listening to my voice my next instruction...

With your will power move to the sensations of relaxation up to your lower back, middle and your upper back... mindfully become aware of any sensations... perhaps the sensation of your relaxed muscles touching the back of the chair or the surface of the bed...

Feel relaxation covering your belly as it rises and falls every time you breath in and out... moving up to your chest... **feeling so relaxed now...**

Relaxation feeling travel up your shoulders and down to your hands all the way to your fingertips... feel your shoulders, arms, forearms, hands and fingers **being completely relaxed... mindfully observe relaxation being present in your upper body and intentionally double your relaxation as you become aware of that pleasant feeling of deeply relaxed muscles...**

With your mindful attention follow relaxation going to your neck... jaw... face... and head... Feel all the tiny muscles around your mouth and eyes beginning to get softer... your whole face becomes smooth and very... **very relaxed right now**...

Finally, allow your mindful awareness to expand and become aware of your entire body from the top of your head down to the bottom of your toes... **completely relaxed**... all now being connected with the natural rhythm of your breathing...

Imagine your breath going through your whole body... from the top of your head down to the bottom of your toes... **making you feel deep calmness and tranquility**... inhale deeply and observe mindfully your breath going from the top of your head down to the bottom of your toes as you inhale… and your breath going from the bottom of your toes all the way up to the top of your head as you exhale… **and double your relaxation**…

If it happens you notice some of your thoughts or emotions… simply acknowledge them for a brief moment and shift your focus back to your breath that is going from the top of your head down to the bottom of your toes and back…

Now, as you are being completely aware of this present moment and mindful…

Recognize any sensation that you have in your body as you think about food in your rapid weight loss diet plan…

As you start thinking about food notice, do you feel hungry, thirsty or maybe not feeling hungry... notice what your mind is telling you… what would you like to eat or drink right now…? Pay attention to your desires or even cravings… and just like you did before with your thoughts and emotions… allow those sensations, desires and cravings to be there… **passively observe them with your relaxed mindful awareness… and let them come and go…**

Imagine **food that is in your rapid weight loss diet plan** right in front of you and imagine looking at this food with great curiosity... notice all the colors, shapes and smells…

And as you are looking at all these food, realize how grateful you are to have so many options to **create wonderful, nutrition and low calorie meals and snack for yourself** to fulfill your plans and **start rapidly losing weight**…

Bring your focus back to your breath that is going from the top of your head down to the bottom of your toes… and notice how **your awareness of this present moment becomes stronger…**

All of these foods **create different meals and snacks that are delicious, nutritious and low in calories and size…** make the size of your meals and snacks smaller than usual **and by doing so reduce your daily calorie intake…**

Choose your favorite meal from your diet plan and take one piece of food and bring it closer to your face… smell and mindfully become aware of all sensations and everything else going on inside your body and mind…

Allow all sensations, thoughts, emotions to be there and simply **observe them with your relaxed and passive awareness…**

Gently place that piece of food into your mouth…. And let it rest there for a second or two without chewing or swallowing it… allow it to be there as you notice the flavor and texture… and above all… **notice your self-control…**

Bring your focus back to your breath that is going from the top of your head down to the bottom of your toes... **and notice how your awareness of this present moment and your self-control becomes even stronger...**

Start slowly to chew this piece of food, and mindfully become aware of all the flavors and aware of all muscles being involved in chewing...

Pay attention to the sounds you make as you are chewing, and once you are satisfied with experiencing all the flavors, swallow this peace of food and notice the taste that may linger in your mouth...

Bring your focus back to your breath that is going from the top of your head down to the bottom of your toes... **and notice how your awareness of this present moment, your self-control, and your satisfaction becomes even stronger as you mindfully choose and decide to eat small amounts of delicious, nutritious and low calorie food...**

In a moment, I am going to start counting down from five to one... and when you hear me saying "one" **you will become fully awake, aware and alert... ready to mindfully enjoy your diet plan...**

Five... **slowly starting to come back**... four... becoming aware of the position of your relaxed body... three... becoming aware of space around you... two... **your energy and motivation are growing stronger**... one... open your eyes, stretch your body as you become **fully awake, aware and alert... ready to mindfully enjoy your diet plan.**

Stop Self-Sabotage Eating

(30 minutes)

Hello, and welcome to your Rapid Weight Loss Hypnosis Program For Women, which will help you on your journey by installing the most useful behaviors, motivation, and thinking patterns for rapid weight loss.

This is your eleventh hypnotic lesson and it will help you to **stop self-sabotage eating by becoming in charge of your emotions, so you can achieve your ideal weight and health goals much easier.**

In your tenth hypnotic lesson, you learned how to extend your mindfulness from your meditation practice into your normal waking life and be more mindful while eating. Practicing mindfulness with your diet plan will help you reduce calories and have greater control over your choices.

This hypnotic lesson will help you with having more control over your emotions, that are part of the decision-making process, **so you can effortlessly achieve your rapid weight loss goals.**

Let's begin now…

Find a nice and cozy place where you won't be disturbed… and before you become completely absorbed with the sound of my voice… make yourself comfortable enough to go **into a state of relaxation... you can sit or lie down…** and close your eyes…

This rapid weight loss mindset begins to activate as soon as you intentionally **start to relax and calm yourself down**... **just like right now** and by realizing… that when **you fill your mind with relaxing thoughts…** any time of the day… **you will feel more centered and in control of your emotions…**

Make final adjustments... and shift your focus and follow your breathing... observe mindfully... air going inside and filing your lungs until that point it starts to slowly go out through your nose or mouth...

Make yourself comfortable, and take a deep breath in, to a count of three seconds… one… two… three, hold it for three seconds… two… one… **and let go into relaxation…** take another deep breath through your nose… one… two…three… hold it for three seconds… two… one and **double your relaxation now**… as you gently exhale…

That's right, just like that… **relax** and allow your breathing to happen on its own… no effort needed…

simply be aware of your breath... completely
calm...

Take a deep breath in, to a count of three seconds...
one... two... three, hold it for three seconds... two...
one... **and let go into relaxation...**

Take another deep breath through your nose...
one... two...three... hold it for three seconds...
two... one and **double your relaxation now**... as
you gently exhale...
Continue breathing at a steady pace.... just like that...
and allow the air moving in and out of your lungs
and belly to **deepen your relaxation**...

Become aware of all internal and external sounds...
and begin to shift your focus from outside sounds to
your internal experience of sounds you hear... and
**sense relaxation starting to fill your body and
mind**... If it happens that your mind creates images
associated with sounds you hear, acknowledge them
and bring back your attention to your breathing and
pleasant sounds of this hypnotic lesson.... and
continue to **observe relaxation feelings...**

Now as you are noticing sounds you can also listen
to my voice, that is guiding you **into a more relaxed
state of mind**... and as you become aware of your
relaxation **you can feel relaxation somewhere in
your body**... maybe your head... or shoulders...

arms or legs… locate the relaxation inside your body… and once you become aware of it… **allow that relaxation feeling to spread and fill your entire body…**

If you find your mind wandering as **you deepen your relaxation**… acknowledge that too for a moment… and without judgment bring your focus back to your breathing and continue your journey by listening to my voice my next instruction…

In a moment I am going to start counting down from five to one... and when you hear me saying "one" **you will completely let go of any remaining tension... negative emotions and thoughts…** spontaneously in your way... **and find yourself going deeper and deeper into relaxation**

Five... **going deeper into relaxation**... four**... letting go of any tension**... three... **letting go of negative emotions**... two... **stopping self-sabotage**... one... **spontaneously in your way… go deeper and deeper into relaxation… that's it just like that…**

Continue to drift of deeper and deeper into relaxation.... and imagine yourself in a safe and secure place.... a peaceful and quiet .... a place without any distractions... just allow your mind to come up with a safe and secure place.... a place that is **free of distractions and unwanted thoughts....**

place of pure positive intentions…. a place that brings forth feelings of fulfillment and joy…

If you have several places on your mind… choose the one that is brightest… and that includes positive feelings…

Step inside this place so you can begin to experience a pleasant positive atmosphere of this place…. feel safe… at peace… feel the comfort… the feelings of fulfillment and joy…

Allow yourself to experience whatever memories or thoughts come into your mind as you are experiencing the positive atmosphere in this safe and secure place… distractions free… and notice all those comforting and pleasant memories and thoughts… observe everything around you in this safe and secure place…. listen to the sounds… check if there are any smells or aromas… reach out and touch whatever is in front of you… feel the texture… as you allow yourself to pretend as if you are physically here in this place…

By pretending that you are here in this place you'll **notice that those feelings of safety, peace, comfort, fulfillment and joy are intensified… becoming stronger… imprinting in your intention to stop self-sabotage eating… imprinting deep within your mind and heart… willpower to stop any kind of self-sabotage… as you progress into**

an even more deeply relaxed state of mind and body now... feeling very, very relaxed...

Whenever you think about this safe and secure place, **you'll find yourself experiencing all pleasant feelings immediately... and you may even choose notice those feelings making your intention stronger... to stop self -sabotage eating... so you can achieve your rapid weight loss goals much easier...**

Feel free to enjoy this place whenever you desire... and you may notice, in time, that your **enjoyment here is increasing your willpower to stop any kind of self-sabotage...**

Enjoy this safe and secure place for a few moments and **fill your mind and body with only positive intentions... that will allow you to achieve your weight and health goals faster than before...**

Give yourself permission to enjoy positivity that comes with this place... and notice how easy it is for you to objectively feel and experience all emotions when you feel calmness... notice how it easy for you to recognize emotions that are stimulating self-sabotaging behaviors... and notice **how easy it becomes for you to interrupt those emotions with your strong intention and willpower to stop self-sabotage...**

In fact, whenever you notice any emotion that encourages any kind of self-sabotage you will think of your safe and secure place, **intensify feelings of determination to rapidly lose weight that you are feeling now…. And immediately stop self-sabotage of any kind… including stopping self-sabotage eating…**

You can come to visit this place as much as you want to… **and the more you think about this place the stronger your intention and willpower becomes to lose weight and achieve your health goals…**

All you have to do is take a few deep breaths, close your eyes and think of this safe and secure place... and as soon as you have it in your mind, you'll instantly experience all the positive feelings of peace… **all the safety… all the comfort… and all the fulfillment and joy…**

Enjoy this amazing safe place now **and relax even more than before... as you feel your intention and willpower to stop self-sabotage eating become stronger… and find yourself rapidly losing weight…**

In a moment, I am going to start counting down from five to one... and when you hear me saying "one" **you will become fully awake, aware and alert… ready to have more control over your emotions…**

Five... **slowly starting to come back**... four... becoming aware of the position of your relaxed body... three... becoming aware of space around you... two... **your energy and motivation are growing stronger**... one... open your eyes, stretch your body as you become **fully awake, aware and alert... you are now ready to have more control over your emotions.**

Cravings Gastric Band

(30 minutes)

Hello, and welcome to your Rapid Weight Loss Hypnosis Program For Women, which will help you on your journey by installing the most useful behaviors, motivation, and thinking patterns for rapid weight loss.

This is your twelfth hypnotic lesson and it will help you to **install a mental gastric band for all your craving, so you can achieve your ideal weight and health goals much easier.**

In your eleventh hypnotic lesson, you learned how to have more control over your emotions and make your intentions and willpower much much stronger to stop any kind of self-sabotage behavior. This control will make your decisions more aligned with your weight and health goals.

This hypnotic lesson will assist you with that nagging craving that might come from time to time so you are prepared to meet that challenge, **and so you can effortlessly achieve your rapid weight loss goals.**

Let's begin now…

Find a nice and cozy place where you won't be disturbed… and before you become completely absorbed with the sound of my voice… make yourself comfortable enough to go **into a state of relaxation... you can sit or lie down…** and close your eyes…

This rapid weight loss mindset begins to activate as soon as you intentionally **start to relax and calm yourself down**... **just like right now** and by realizing… that when **you fill your mind with relaxing thoughts…** any time of the day… **you will feel having more choices and be capable of overcoming any challenge…**

Make final adjustments... and start to focus and follow your breathing... observe with your passive awareness... air going inside and filing your lungs until that point it starts to slowly go out through your nose or mouth...

Make yourself comfortable, and take a deep breath in, to a count of three seconds… one… two… three, hold it for three seconds… two… one… **and let go into relaxation…** take another deep breath through your nose… one… two…three… hold it for three seconds… two… one and **double your relaxation now**… as you gently exhale…

That's right, just like that… **relax** and allow your breathing to happen on its own…

Now, as you listen to my voice, you can also notice other relaxing sounds of this hypnotic lesson… and as you become aware of other relaxing sounds **you can feel relaxation somewhere in your body**… maybe your head… or shoulders… arms or legs… and once you become aware of it… **allow that relaxation feeling to spread and fill your entire body…**

Enjoy that relaxation feeling as you think about the position of your body right now…. notice how can you make yourself more comfortable **and double your relaxation**…. as soon as you find a way to relax even deeper…. **make yourself at ease… and become still right now…**

That comfort and stillness allow you to scan your entire body more easily... from head to toes… and from your toes to your head… and as you scan your body with your awareness... just like that... I want you to **notice all your muscles starting to relax...** notice all muscles in your feet... **getting relaxed**.... muscles in your calves... **getting relaxed**... muscles in your thighs... **your lower body is now completely relaxed..**

Instruct all the muscles in your torso to **relaxed**...
your chest muscles... **relax**.... your arms and hands...
relax... your back... **relax**... your neck... **relax**...your
head... **relax**....

Relaxation spreads across your face... muscles on
your chin.... mouth... chicks... nose... and all the tiny
muscles around your eyes.... and forehead... all
getting very.... **very relaxed now**...

Your entire body is now deeply relaxed and all that
is left for you to do is to allow yourself to install a
mental gastric band to reduce all cravings...

Choose a color that you associate with protection and
healing.... a peaceful color of your choice... allow
different peaceful colors to gently float through your
mind until you feel a special connection with one
color that is radiating with the meaning of protection
and healing...

Once you choose this peaceful color imagine it
everywhere around you... imagine that you are
inside a beautiful, protective sphere... and give
yourself permission to feel that connection with your
color... notice what it feels like protection and
healing power caressing your body...

To make this feeling stronger, I would like you to
imagine your color becoming brighter and more
vibrant... and as you do that **notice your feeling of**

being protected and feeling of healing getting stronger…

Imagine your sphere growing… make it bigger... and observe all the **good feelings within you to become two times stronger**... the more you sphere of your protective and healing color becoming bigger... the better you feel…

Notice your color covering each part of your relaxed body… feeling protected…

Feel the color gently covering your face... and your skin absorbs that protective and healing color just like a rejuvenating lotion…

Feel your protective and healing color entering your body… to **create a defense mechanism against all cravings…**

Feel your neck absorbing the color… feel the area around your shoulders... absorbing your color… as **you feel comfort and relaxation deepens…**

Protective and healing color first removes all the stress and all remaining tension... disappearing from your mind and body... and as you experience this relief, notice how easy it becomes for you to **allow the installation of a mental gastric band that will reduce your craving so you can start rapidly lose weight and achieve your ideal weight and health goals…**

And as your body keeps absorbing all the protective and healing powers of your color, the second thing that is starting to happen right now is that **your color removes any feelings such as guilt, loneliness, anger, and emptiness...**

Protective and healing **color is now removing all negativity from your mind and body... leaving you with a calm mind and a deeply relaxed body...**

Allow your mind and body to fully accept this protective and healing color... allow the color to freely flow through your mind and body and to find all locations where you feel your cravings manifest...

Breathe in that wonderful color from your protective and healing sphere... and breathe in all the defense mechanisms against cravings that come with this wonderful healing color... and with each breath in **allow yourself to have all the protection you need to stay on your course and achieve your weight and health goals...**

Inhaling and exhaling... breathing deeply and easily... filling your lungs with your protective and healing **color causes you to feel even more relaxed...**

Your steady and relaxed breathing allows your color to flow through every part of your mind and body... filling every cell, every nerve, every muscle.... freely flowing through your bloodstream... through every joint and bone of your body... **refreshing and rejuvenating your mind and body... easily finding locations of your cravings** such as your stomach… your mouth… your tongue… your thought… or any other location inside your body… **removing all cravings as soon as manifest...**

From now on, if it happens you feel any kind of craving, your protective and healing **color will immediately locate the part of your body with craving sensations… and remove that feeling and restore your mind and body to perfect calmness... filling you with peace, health and happiness... that allows you to effortlessly pursue your weight loss and health goals...**

From this moment forward, every time you think or become aware of your protective and healing color you will start feeling amazing...

From this moment forward, every time you experience any kind of craving… **your protective and healing color will automatically remove that feeling or any sensations from your mind and body…**

Sometimes it will happen so fast you would be able to notice it, and other times you will **consciously use your color to remove any cravings…**

Your mental gastric band to reduce cravings is now completely installed… and you might find yourself being surprised how much more choice you have now to **reduce cravings and stick to your diet plan...**

In a moment, I am going to start counting down from five to one... and when you hear me saying "one" **you will become fully awake, aware and alert... ready to mindfully enjoy your diet plan...**

Five... **slowly starting to come back**... four... becoming aware of the position of your relaxed body... three... becoming aware of space around you... two... **your energy and motivation are growing stronger**... one... open your eyes, stretch your body as you become **fully awake, aware and alert... ready to mindfully enjoy your diet plan.**

Water Weight Loss

(30 minutes)

Hello, and welcome to your Rapid Weight Loss Hypnosis Program For Women, which will help you on your journey by installing the most useful behaviors, motivation, and thinking patterns for rapid weight loss.

This is your thirteenth hypnotic lesson and it will help you to **speed up your metabolism and burn fat by associating your weight loss with water, so you can achieve your ideal weight and health goals much easier.**

In your twelfth hypnotic lesson, you learned how to deal with any kind of cravings in a healthy way that will allow you to stick to your diet plans and your new more beneficial lifestyle. Interrupting your impulses and taking more appropriate actions will lead you to create more healthier habits, and with more healthier habits you will have a more healthier life.

This hypnotic lesson will use water as a symbol of your strong desire to have a healthier lifestyle, **so**

you can effortlessly achieve your rapid weight loss goals.

Let's begin now…

Find a nice and cozy place that is free from any distractions… and start to focus completely one the sound of my voice… make yourself comfortable enough to go **into a state of relaxation… you can sit or lie down…** and close your eyes…

This rapid weight loss mindset begins to activate as soon as you intentionally **start to relax and calm yourself down… just like right now** and by realizing… that when **you fill your mind with relaxing thoughts…** any time of the day… **you will notice your metabolism improving…**

So as soon as you are ready to **start creating the reality you want to live right now…** simply shift your focus to your breathing… Notice the air going inside your lungs and going out… That's it… now inhale deeply and slowly …. and exhale… gently and slowly… **relaxing into a more positive state of mind…**

Breathe deeply and slowly… at a pace that is just perfect for you… effortlessly… **becoming more and more relaxed…** with each inhalation… and with each exhalation… going deeper and deeper into a complete calmness of the mind and stillness of the body…

In a moment I am going to guide you through breathing techniques, where I will ask you to inhale for four seconds, hold your breath for five seconds and exhale for six seconds. This breathing pattern will help you **deepen your relaxation two times more than so far** …There is no effort needed from you in any way... just follow my voice... al let your body do the rest…

Begin with inhaling slowly to a count of four... three... two... one and hold that breath to a count of five seconds.... four... three... two...one, and slowly exhale to a count of six **as you release all nervousness**.... five ...four... three... two... one **completely relaxed now... calm mind... still body…**

Again, start inhaling to a count of four... three... two... one, hold it for five seconds.... four… three... two... one **and let go into relaxation as you release all remaining tension all the way down... all the way down... That's right... just like that... completely call... perfectly still... deeply relaxed…**

Now that **you are experiencing a deep level of relaxation and awareness**… allow yourself to think of the nearest door to you…

Out there you might know where this door will lead you… but inside your mind… this door can lead you to many different places… and one of those places is a quiet room… and in this room you can associate anything from your environment with your goals… associations that will **constantly direct your conscious and unconscious focus toward your rapid weight loss…**

Go ahead now imagine walking toward that door… grab the doorknob and turn it… open the door and enter that quiet room…

Once inside, notice a nice big soft chair in the middle of the room… sit down in this comfy chair and allow yourself to **go into an even deeper state of relaxation…**

You are in this quiet room for one reason only, and that is to **train your mind and body to naturally improve metabolism and burn fat…** you are here because you want **rapidly lose weight, stay relaxed and achieve your health goals….**

After this session you will move through your days and evenings **feeling more relaxed … calm and at peace… knowing that your body is working with you and for you…**

Begin to think and remember all kinds of different sounds of water… think about how the water feels on different temperatures… and what sensations you experience as you drink water…

Decide that you will **associate water with your weight loss plan** from now on, and whenever you see or even hear the sound of water, you'll immediately **allow your subconscious to make all necessary changes and improve your metabolism…**

Every time you see water in your nearest surroundings, this will **automatically trigger your mind and body to start focusing on improving your metabolism and burn fat…** everything that reminds you of water will set that trigger on…

Whenever you see a body of water... whether it's a brook, an ocean, a river, or even a swimming pool... **you immediately start to relax and improve your metabolism...** When you hear or even think about water, **you begin to relax, and your body starts to work and to burn fat... making your rapid weight lose more easier for you…**

Hearing the sound of rain, or a fountain, or shower, **triggers your mind and body to go into a relaxed state where you can naturally start improving your metabolism in many ways…**

If it happens by any chance that you ever begin to feel anxious, worried, concerned, or stressful, for whatever reason, start thinking about water... any kind of water... and you'll **immediately wash away all your anxieties, worries, concerns and stress... become completely relax... and that will allow your mind and body to function more effectively ... so you can spontaneously and effortlessly lose weight rapidly....**

When you are relaxed everything works better... your mindset is better... you feel more energy inside your body... and your body uses that energy to functions better... your body uses this relaxed energy to **improve your health in many ways... including speeding up your metabolism to burn fat more easily...**

At this moment **you are deciding to start drinking more water** on a regular basis... and **the more water you drink, the better you feel...**

Every glass of water you drink makes you feel relaxed... because water can collect all negativity, all worries and simply wash them away...

Whenever you drink or imagine that you are drinking a glass of water you will **automatically wash away all negativity and worries from your mind and body...** and that will allow your mind and body to function more effectively ... so **you can**

spontaneously and effortlessly lose weight rapidly….

If you find yourself feeling hungry but know you are not supposed to consume any food at that moment, you will remember to have a glass of fresh water… and that will **wash away your feeling of hunger and fill your body with energy that your subconscious mind can use to improve all the functions of your body including improving your metabolism and burning fat, so you can effortlessly achieve your weight and health goals…**

Water is now your best ally for rapid weight loss… it will constantly remind you of your healthier choices… so you can create the reality you want to live right now… and **fully accept your new healthy lifestyle…**

Allow powerful symbols of water to completely integrate with your whole being… **create meaningful associations that will trigger your mind and body to focus on improving your metabolism and burn fat naturally…** each time you see, hear or drink water your body will know what to do and bring you closer toward your ideal weight…

Imagine drinking a glass of fresh water as you **allow yourself to preserve all the learnings, insights and positive associations from this hypnotic lesson...**

In a moment, I am going to start counting down from five to one... and when you hear me saying "one" **you will become fully awake, aware and alert... ready to rapidly lose weight with water...**

Five... **slowly starting to come back**... four... becoming aware of the position of your relaxed body... three... becoming aware of space around you... two... **your energy and motivation are growing stronger**... one... open your eyes, stretch your body as you become **fully awake, aware and alert... ready to rapidly lose weight with water.**

Eat healthy Food and Forget Junk Food

(30 minutes)

Hello, and welcome to your Rapid Weight Loss Hypnosis Program For Women, which will help you on your journey by installing the most useful behaviors, motivation, and thinking patterns for rapid weight loss.

This is your fourteenth hypnotic lesson and it will help you to **consciously become aware of the consequences that come with bad and good decisions, so you can achieve your ideal weight and health goals much easier.**

In your thirteenth hypnotic lesson, you learned how to associate water with your weight and health goals. These powerful associations will keep your conscious and unconscious mind focused on your goals and you will constantly progress toward your success.

This hypnotic lesson will present two possible futures ahead of you from which the only one can become your reality. In here you can safely face all the consequences of your choices and make the right decision today, **so you can effortlessly achieve your rapid weight loss goals.**

Let's begin now…

Find a nice and cozy place where you won't be disturbed… and before you become completely absorbed with my voice and start following my instruction… make yourself comfortable enough to go **into a state of relaxation, tranquility and peace… you can sit or lie down…** and close your eyes…

This rapid weight loss mindset begins to activate as soon as you intentionally **start to relax and calm yourself down… just like right now** and by realizing… that when **you fill your mind with relaxing thoughts…** any time of the day… **you will create all necessary conditions to make good decisions and the right choices…**

So as soon as you are ready to **start letting go of tension and make yourself comfortable…** simply shift your focus to your breathing… Notice the air going inside your lungs and going out… That's it… now take a deep breath in…. and let it go… gently… **relaxing into a more peaceful state of mind…**

Breath slowly and deeply… at a pace that is just perfect for you… without effort… **becoming more**

and more at peace… with each breath in… and becoming more and more relaxed with each breath out…

In a moment I am going to guide you through breathing techniques, where I will ask you to inhale for four seconds, hold your breath for five seconds and exhale for six seconds. This breathing pattern will help you **become more relaxed** ...No effort needed... just follow my voice...

Begin with inhaling slowly to a count of four... three... two... one and hold that breath to a count of five seconds.... four... three... two...one, and slowly exhale to a count of six **as you release all the tension**.... five ...four... three... two... one **completely relaxed now…**

Again, start inhaling to a count of four... three... two... one, hold it for five seconds.... four… three... two... one **and let go into relaxation as you release all remaining tension all the way down... all the way down... That's right... just like that...**

Make your body lighter with light… I would like you to imagine that there is a brilliant light above your head...

Feel the presence of that brilliant light above the top of your head.... and allow that brilliant light to cover your entire body... starting with your head... imagine every inch on your head covered with that brilliant light... **facial and scalp muscles smooth out and relax and light on your skin makes you feel lighter…**

This brilliant light is now covering your neck... gently moving toward your shoulders... spreading over every inch of your arms... all the way to your fingertips... **your shoulders and arms are very light… almost weightless… deeply relaxed…**

Notice how your back, chest and stomach muscles **become soft and limp as soon as you see and feel that brilliant light covering your upper body...**

Continue to **relax and go deeper and deeper as you feel yourself becoming lighter and lighter…** and follow that brilliant light with your awareness as it goes down toward your legs... making them so relaxed… very light… almost weightless…

Your imagination is very powerful, and your mind can create many logical predictions of your future, quite accurately, with enough facts…

For example, we are all aware, and it is a proven fact, that junk food is not good for our health… We also know, exercise or any other physical activity is important for our wellbeing…

So let's have a look and see what kind of future your mind can logically predict with these two facts…

Imagine now that you're doing what you know it's not good for you…. in your everyday life there is enough space for all the junk food you can eat and no room for any activity

See yourself doing this day after day, week after week and month after month… eating only junk food and moving your body only for the basic needs…

Now jump forward two – three - four years into the future…

Look around you… see where you are and notice your surroundings, hear all the sounds… and find yourself in the future after the number of years of eating only junk food and not exercising…

What would really happen to you, to your body and to your health? How would you feel in that future knowing that you probably add more weight… notice what emotions are there in that future…? I guess **they are not pleasant at all**… Is this how you want your future to be? Well don't worry… it's not going to look like that… **it will probably get even worse**… because this is only two three years from now… but **after ten years it will be devastating…**

And as your mind presents you this possible future, based on logic and proven facts notice **how much power you actually have right now to change that...**

And the best part is that you don't have to do that much all at once**... it all comes down to a single step that you are about to make...**

A decision to go left or right... and choose between junk food and healthy food.... Choose between inactivity and activity...

Let's have a look at what your mind would predict now when **you make the right decision and choose to eat healthy food and exercise...**

Imagine now that **you're doing what you know is good for you**.... in your everyday life there is only space for healthy food and plenty of physical activities including exercising...

See yourself doing this day after day, week after week and month after month... eating only healthy food and being super active...

Now jump forward two – three - four years into the future...

Look around you... see where you are and notice your surroundings, hear all the sounds... and find yourself in the future after the number of years of eating only healthy food and exercising every day...

What would happen to you in this future… what would happen to your body and to your health? How would you feel in that future knowing that you have an ideal weight and perfect health? Notice what emotions are there in that future…? Feels good doesn't it?

Take it all in… **experience joy, happiness and fulfillment… knowing that even better future awaits you in ten years from now… feel all the benefits of your success…**

As you experience these benefits, **you know that you made the right choice**... and all of these amazing things are happening to you just because you made that one small step today…. **toward the right decision…**

This beautiful and bright future ahead of you totally pushes away that other unpleasant future… **making you completely forget about all the junk food…**

This logical prediction of your mind allows you to **be smart with every choice you make,** and in time **it gets easier and easier for you to make the right choices… because It's easy to make choices that are beneficial for you today and tomorrow…**

Starting today, follow your good choice **and find yourself doing whatever is necessary to achieve your rapid weight loss goals and perfect health…**

In a moment, I am going to start counting down from five to one... and when you hear me saying "one" **you will become fully awake, aware and alert... ready to make good decisions and the right choices for your health...**

Five... **slowly starting to come back**... four... becoming aware of the position of your relaxed body... three... becoming aware of space around you... two... **your energy and motivation are growing stronger**... one... open your eyes, stretch your body as you become **fully awake, aware and alert... ready to make good decisions and the right choices for your health.**

Hypnosis Affirmations

(30 minutes)

Hello, and welcome to your Rapid Weight Loss Hypnosis Program For Women, which will help you on your journey by installing the most useful behaviors, motivation, and thinking patterns for rapid weight loss.

This is your fifteenth hypnotic lesson and it will help you to **plant some powerful seeds in the form of hypnosis affirmations that will make beliefs about yourself stronger, so you can achieve your ideal weight and health goals much easier.**

In your fourteenth hypnotic lesson, you learned how to use logical predictions of the future and see possible consequences of your decision and choices that you make today. This ability to safely explore outcomes of your decisions will allow you to make the best choices for your health and overall wellbeing.

This hypnotic lesson is all about building your belief system stronger, **so you can effortlessly achieve your rapid weight loss goals.**

Let's begin now…

Find a nice and cozy place where you won't be disturbed… and before you become completely absorbed with the sound of my voice… make yourself comfortable enough to go **into a state of relaxation... you can sit or lie down...** and close your eyes…

This rapid weight loss mindset begins to activate as soon as you intentionally **start to relax and calm yourself down**... **just like right now** and by realizing… that when **you fill your mind with relaxing thoughts…** any time of the day… **you will feel more energized, motivated and capable of facing any challenge…**

When you listen to hypnotic lessons like this you are practicing to **passively observe your thoughts, feelings, and sensations in your body**. You also **maintain your focus on what is important and become mindful or develop a relaxed awareness** of your inner world and surroundings…

Most of the time when we set a goal, there are certain things on our mind that we need to do or expectations that we need to meet… **you might organize our time perfectly,** but do you **set yourself up for success by choosing to believe in yourself** ?

One of the healthiest things you can do before you start your daily activities is to **check your belief system and see if there is any adjustments needed...**

You might ask yourself, how would you know is there is any adjustment needed, and the answer is simple... if you are not feeling absolutely confident that you got this thing that you are pursuing, or if you are not what will the outcome be... or if you are having trouble seeing yourself having what you want... if you are not totally motivated to achieve your goal... those are the usual signs that let you know is time to check what you believe in...

You are here, listening to this program, because you are a loving person... and also, you are here because **you want to have stronger more empowering beliefs about yourself**... belief system that allows you to be **stress free**... a positive attitude that reminds you that **you can accomplish anything you want**... because **you deserve to have good health and feel great...**

Make all the adjustments... and start to focus and follow your breathing... **observe mindfully...** air going inside and filing your lungs until that point it starts to slowly go out through your nose or mouth...

Take a deep breath in, to a count of three seconds…
one… two… three, hold it for three seconds… two…
one… **and let go into relaxation…**

Take another deep breath through your nose…
one… two…three… hold it for three seconds…
two… one and **double your relaxation now**… as
you gently exhale…
Continue breathing at a steady pace…. just like that…
and allow the air moving in and out of your lungs
and belly to **deepen your relaxation**…

Notice how sounds of this hypnosis lesson creating
some **pleasant sensations inside you**…. and as that
sound travels through your ears allow that **pleasant
sensation of relaxation** start spreading and fill every
cell in your head and face.

**Feel that tingling sensation of relaxation in every
cell… getting stronger and stronger… making you
even more relaxed… as you double the comfort
you are experiencing right now…**

And because all your cells are connected… and share
the same experience of **comfort…. and relaxation…**
that means… all other cells in your body can **relax
right now…**

That pleasant sensation of tranquility and peace… is
sending the signal to all the cells in your body…
relax…. connect with yourself…. connect to your

core beliefs... starting from your head and face... notice how this signal travels down your neck.... **filing every cell with relaxation....** down your shoulders and arms.... **pleasant tingling sensation of comfort.....** your chest.... back... and stomach... **know how to relax....** just by observing and allowing the signal of relaxation to keep spreading down your legs and feet and all the way back to your head.... creating that **continuous cycle of tranquility and peace inside your body right now...** **giving you opportunity to see what adjustments you need to make in order to successfully accomplish your rapid weight loss goals...**

If pleasant sounds that you hear can make **you feel more relaxed....** in the same way **empowering beliefs can make you feel more energized and motivated** to accomplish anything you like... including your goal to **rapidly lose weight...**

And as your breath follow this **continuous cycle of tranquility and peace in your body...** you can notice that you are starting to create more and more empowering beliefs**... and the more empowering beliefs you have, the more confident and motivated you feel... the more confident and motivated you to feel the more your certainty becomes stronger... and the more your certainty**

becomes stronger more easier it becomes for you to achieve your rapid weight loss goals...

Imagine being in a safe space... it can be indoors or outdoors... familiar or imagined place... in any case, **you feel very safe being at this place and you feel very relaxed**... perhaps you can find a nice and cozy spot in this safe place where you can sit and **make yourself comfortable for a moment...**

And as you sit... notice **how your relaxation deepens**... and **your confidence and motivation grow bigger inside you... convincing you that you can achieve anything you want...**

As you are feeling your confidence and motivation getting stronger and stronger... suddenly you see a small paper scroll next to you... kind of scroll that is used for important messages...

Naturally, you reach out and take the paper scroll in your hand and open it... only to see **the most powerful empowering beliefs inside**... beliefs that will **increase your confidence and motivation... enhance your inner vision so you can clearly see yourself being successful...**

Read these powerful beliefs, repeat them inside your mind after me... and each time you read and repeat any belief... imagine that you are saying it louder and louder...

**I am happily achieving my rapid weight loss
goals!**

Repeat it much louder inside your mind…

**I now clearly see myself at my ideal weight in
perfect health!**

Repeat it louder and hear this belief echoing into
distance everywhere around you…

**I deserve to have a slim, healthy and attractive
body!**

Turn the volume up… let your voice reach all
corners of the Earth…

**I celebrate my own power to make choices
around food!**

Repeated even louder than before…

One more powerful belief…

**I am the creator of my future and the driver of
my mind! I will succeed!**

Repeat it in your mind so loudly that the whole
universe can hear you…

As soon as you repeat these empowering beliefs **notice how much more confidence, motivation and certainty you have...**

Allow yourself for these powerful seeds to grow even bigger and stronger... and create an unstoppable belief system that will lead you to your desired destination...

Passively observe with your relaxed awareness that confidence and motivation **fill your mind and body and clearing the road ahead of you...** as you slowly start coming back...

In a moment, I am going to start counting down from five to one... and when you hear me saying "one" **you will become fully awake, aware and alert... feeling confident and super motivated to achieve your rapid weight loss goals...**

Five... **slowly starting to come back**... four... becoming aware of the position of your relaxed body... three... becoming aware of space around you... two... **your energy and motivation are growing stronger**... one... open your eyes, stretch your body as you become **fully awake, aware and alert... feeling confident and super motivated to achieve your rapid weight loss goals.**

Walking Weight Loss

(30 minutes)

Hello, and welcome to your Rapid Weight Loss Hypnosis Program For Women, which will help you on your journey by installing the most useful behaviors, motivation, and thinking patterns for rapid weight loss.

This is your sixteenth hypnotic lesson and it will help you to **express gratitude toward your amazing body and all the wonderful things your body is capable of, so you can achieve your ideal weight and health goals much easier.**

In your fifteenth hypnotic lesson, you learned how to use your belief system to develop more confidence, motivation and certainty while moving toward your goals. Having empowering belief about yourself and the goal you are pursuing is one of the most important factors for success.

This hypnotic lesson will help you create deeper connection with your subconscious mind by expressing your gratitude toward your body and all its amazing functions and capabilities, **so you can effortlessly achieve your rapid weight loss goals.**

Let's begin now…

Find a nice and cozy place where you won't be disturbed… and before you become completely absorbed with the sound of my voice… make yourself comfortable enough to go **into a state of relaxation... you can sit or lie down…** and close your eyes…

This rapid weight loss mindset begins to activate as soon as you intentionally **start to relax and calm yourself down**... **just like right now** and by realizing… that when **you fill your mind with relaxing thoughts…** any time of the day… **you will feel more energized, motivated and capable of facing any challenge…**

Make any final adjustments... and start to focus and follow your breathing... **observe mindfully...** air going inside and filing your lungs until that point it starts to slowly go out through your nose or mouth... and pay attention to that point where breathing in stops and breathing out begins… a pure moment of silence and stillness of your mind and body…

Mindfully follow the air going in and out through your nose.... slowly inhale.... and exhale.... air going in..... and air going out... **relaxing**… and notice... mindfully... the slight difference in temperature of that air as you let it go out.... going deeper as you focus on your attention on the small area in your trough where you can feel circulation of the air.... and notice all sensations of air going in..... and air going out... and the slight difference in the temperature of that air... **relaxing** each time you inhale... and **relaxing** even deeper every time you exhale....

Observe your breathing mindfully and as you do that notice all the sensations and the way your body makes subtle calm movements... and if it happens that your attention wanders... from one thought to another... just bring your focus back on your breathing and **continue to deepen your relaxation...**

Make your breath even by making your inhalation and exhalation the same... inhale for five seconds and exhale for five seconds... count inside your mind...

Inhaling... one... two... three... four... five... relaxing... Exhaling... one... two... three... four... five... relaxing... Inhaling... one... two... three... four... five... relaxing... Exhaling... one... two... three... four... five... relaxing...

That's right you are doing great.... **feeling very relaxed now...**

I would like you to imagine now that you are going for a walk… feel free to choose any scenery that is enjoyable for you… **chose a path that will lead you to your success**

Inside your mind start walking down that path and whenever you are ready to shift your focus to your body… because we will start **to give thanks to your body for all its incredible functions and capabilities…**

Gratitude is the key emotion to establishing better rapport with your subconscious mind and to create that mutual trust between your consciousness and your subconsciousness…

This gratitude will connect all your desires with your capabilities to successfully accomplish your rapid weight loss goals…

I will guide you to visit various parts of your body, as you are walking through this scenery, down that path of success… and all you have to do is to recognize where you feel the gratitude is coming from… and as soon as you locate the source or resting place of your gratitude, feel the **gratitude fountaining from every cell of your body… allowing you to start losing weight even faster than before…**

Begin at the top of your head and focus on your scalp… Imagine your hairs attached to your scalp…. covering and protecting your head… making you look beautify…

Express your gratitude to your hair for being there to protect your scalp and make you look beautiful…

Become aware of your skull... and **express your gratitude** toward your skull for its amazing shape.... notice how the feeling of gratitude is sending from your skull through all your bones and joints… feeling so relaxed... all the way down…

Feel the gratitude for your skeleton as it gives you support and protection… to **move easily toward your weight loss and health goals…**

Send your gratitude past the skull into your brain.... **give thanks to your brain**.... and **start feeling grateful for all the intelligence you have**… think about all the amazing functions of your brain and what your brain is making you be capable of… and as you do that **express your deep gratitude for having a brain and mind that is dedicated to achieving your weight loss goals…**

Focus on your eyes... and **be thankful for the sense of sight**... and your **ability to see all the benefits of your new healthier lifestyle...** be thankful for being able to see vast beauty ever here around you… be grateful for all the smiling faces you see… **be**

grateful for seeing your smile in the future when you achieve your ideal weight and perfect health…

Keep walking inside your mind, down that path of success… and notice how **walking activity speeds up your process of weight lose…**

Every time you walk your body uses this activity to naturally burn fat… and generate more positive energy…

Now pay attention to your nose... **and thank your nose for the ability to have a sense of smell** which allows you to enjoy the most pleasant aromas… give thanks to this and other abilities of your nose…. **including the ability to smell good opportunities and success ahead of you…**

Think about the perfection of your mouth and tongue**... and thank your mouth for the sense of taste** which allows you to enjoy many different flavors… and **give thanks to your tongue for your ability to speak....**

Allow your consciousness to move toward your throat and your stomach... **express your gratitude** toward your stomach for its digestive capability... ability to extract all the vitamins and minerals from the food that is necessary for your health …

Think of all the organs in your stomach area… think about your liver, pancreas, spleen, gallbladder, small intestine, large intestine… think about all the amazing functions they do… and **thank these organs for the important role they play in everyday weight loss functions of your body….**

As you imagine walking through that pleasant scenery, down the path of success… allow your awareness to visit each of these organs and **thank them once again**… **think about their role in your weight loss… and feel gratitude…**

Think about your kidneys end **feel the gratitude for their function of cleaning your blood of toxins** and wastes from your bloodstream...

Thank your blood veins and arteries for providing circulation of the blood to all parts of your body and feeding your entire body with a powerful imine system...

Now take a deep breath in… and as you shift your focus to your breathing think about your lungs... and **express your gratitude for providing oxygen to your body...**

Visit your heart… **feel deep gratitude for your heart** and it continues beating and pumping blood to all parts of your body non-stop...

And finally think about the skin that covers your body... and **express your gratitude for all the functions of your skin...**

In a moment, I am going to start counting down from five to one... and when you hear me saying "one" **you will become fully awake, aware and alert... ready to lose weight naturally every time you go for a walk...**

Five... **slowly starting to come back**... four... becoming aware of the position of your relaxed body... three... becoming aware of space around you... two... **your energy and motivation are growing stronger**... one... open your eyes, stretch your body as you become **fully awake, aware and alert... ready to lose weight naturally every time you go for a walk.**

Live More Actively

(30 minutes)

Hello, and welcome to your Rapid Weight Loss Hypnosis Program For Women, which will help you on your journey by installing the most useful behaviors, motivation, and thinking patterns for rapid weight loss.

This is your seventeenth hypnotic lesson and it will help you to **start generating more energy and live a life filled with activity, so you can achieve your ideal weight and health goals much easier.**

In your sixteenth hypnotic lesson, you learned how to express your gratitude toward your whole body and your subconscious mind. The level of your success is determined by the strength of your relationship with your subconscious mind and your body, and your desires are now perfectly aligned with your capabilities.

This hypnotic lesson will build upon that strong relationship between your conscious mind and your subconscious mind by communicating your desires more clearly, **so you can effortlessly achieve your rapid weight loss goals.**

Let's begin now...

Find a nice and cozy place where you won't be disturbed... and before you become completely absorbed with the sound of my voice... make yourself comfortable enough to go **into a state of relaxation... you can sit or lie down...** and close your eyes...

This rapid weight loss mindset begins to activate as soon as you intentionally **start to relax and calm yourself down...** **just like right now** and by realizing... that when **you fill your mind with relaxing thoughts...** any time of the day... **you will feel more energized, motivated and capable of facing any challenge...**

As you give yourself permission to deeply relax... start with thinking about all the activities that you enjoy... everyone has their favorite activities... and when we use our time to do our favorite activities that means we can experience fun and joy naturally anytime we choose to do so...

Being active throughout the day when pursuing your weight loss goals allows you to **get there faster and achieve your weight and health goals much quicker...** and that gives you more time to **enjoy the**

journey… go with the flow… and have fun as you rapidly lose weight…

Let's express your desires to your subconscious mind in a more effective way… using your imagery… I would like you to imagine that there is a source of energy above your head...

Feel the presence of that energy source above the top of your head.... and allow that energy to fill up your entire body... starting with your head... imagine every cell in your head filled with that new energy... **activating every cell in your brain to seek fulfilling activities…**

This source of energy is now felling your neck... gently flowing toward your shoulders... your arms... all the way to your fingertips... **and that mild tingling sensation lets you know that you are now energizing your body…**

Notice how your back, chest and stomach muscles **become energized as soon as you become aware of that energy source filling your upper body**...

Follow that energy flow with your awareness as it goes down toward your legs... **filling them with excitement and desire to take immediate action… and start having a more active life…**

All small muscles in your feet are now filled with that energy.... and as your feet **begin to feel more energized**... allow that energy to move upwards.... up your calves and knees... **making your muscles filled with vitality and enthusiasm...** fill that energy in your thighs... experiencing that excitement to take immediate action and have a more active lifestyle…

Energy is moving up your torso... stomach and lower back.... **becoming even more energized...**

And naturally, as energy reaches your chest you take a deep breath in… and fill your lungs with energy... as your upper body evenly distributes that energy across your shoulders and arm all the way to your fingertips.... **and that mild tingling sensation lets you know that you are now energizing your body...** reminding you that you are about to **start living life filled with activities... and achieve your weight and health goals much quicker...**

This will happen on its own... just by **expressing your desires clearly... your subconscious will help you to achieve your weight loss goals...** your body and your subconscious mind will know how to do that for you...

Continue breathing at a steady pace.... just like that... and allow the air moving in and out of your lungs and belly to **deepen your relaxation...**

Imagine that each time you inhale... **action energy fills your head, neck, and chest...** and as you exhale that **action energy spreads through the rest of your body.... just like a wave... filling your head, neck, and chest as you inhale.... and spreads that action energy all over your body as it goes down...** your arms and bally... all the way down your legs and feet.... **filling you with vitality and enthusiasm... allowing you to effortlessly move toward your rapid weight loss goals...**

You know your conscious mind and subconscious mind are parts of your whole being… and that means **you can use your subconscious mind to create the reality of health you want to live...**

The subconscious mind is completely in charge of your body... the way it develops… the way your body moves… and your conscious mind is in charge of your subconscious mind… and that means **you can tell your subconscious mind how to use your body… you can use your mind to improve your body just the way you want it...**

Knowing this, **use your creativity and imagination to create an image of a healthy active body**… start now, and **imagine a healthy body filled with energy and capable of doing all the activities you deep enjoy and you deeply desire... imagine all** these fun activities naturally burning fat... losing extra weight... building your body stronger... capable of doing anything your heart desires...

Allow your mind to show you a mental image of yourself **living an active lifestyle... being healthy and happy... filled with active energy and excitement**... involve all of your senses to make this mental image your reality... notice the way your body moves.... see yourself in a time of your success listen to people giving you compliments about your looks and your level od vibrant health... **every movement of your body feels so light... effortless... graceful...**

Imagine yourself eating healthy foods you enjoy and explaining to others how your healthy food choices got you where you are right now... **in perfect health with your ideal weight**... hear yourself explaining how this delicious healthy food helps your body to **have more energy and stamina... allowing you to live a very active lifestyle filled with happiness...**

Enjoy these conversations and feelings of vitality and enthusiasm... and intensify your feeling by carefully listening to these truth statements...

You are in perfect health... You are filled with active energy... You love your everyday physical activities... Every day in every way you are becoming more and more active...

Your desires are now clearly expressed to your subconscious mind… and your subconscious mind will now start to **make all necessary changes to make this active lifestyle your reality... allow your subconscious mind to make it happen... expect it to happen... and be the first witness when it happens...**

Your subconscious mind loves to follow your instructions and is working around the clock to **make this happen for you**... giving you all the necessary support... generating and **creating endless amounts of energy... positivity and good vibrations so you can achieve your rapid weight loss goals effortlessly... faster than you ever** imagined…

You know how this works... **and you believe your subconscious mind** to make all these changes for you... because **you have a deep connection with your whole being** and know the power of your subconscious mind… enjoy this feeling and **allow all changes to happen spontaneously... as you**

become someone who lives a healthy lifestyle filled with activities...

In a moment, I am going to start counting down from five to one... and when you hear me saying "one" **you will become fully awake, aware and alert... ready to live a more exciting and healthy life filled with activity...**

Five... **slowly starting to come back**... four... becoming aware of the position of your relaxed body... three... becoming aware of space around you... two... **your energy and motivation are growing stronger**... one... open your eyes, stretch your body as you become **fully awake, aware and alert... ready to live a more exciting and healthy life filled with activity...**

Be More Compassionate to Yourself

(30 minutes)

Hello, and welcome to your Rapid Weight Loss Hypnosis Program For Women, which will help you on your journey by installing the most useful behaviors, motivation, and thinking patterns for rapid weight loss.

This is your eighteenth hypnotic lesson and it will help you to **become a more self-caring and compassionate person to yourself, so you can achieve your ideal weight and health goals much easier.**

In your seventeenth hypnotic lesson, you learned how to express your desires to your subconscious mind regarding all things you want to do in your life, so it can create all necessary changes to make that happen for you. By giving clear instructions and expressing our desires in a way that is respectful toward our whole being allows us to use all of our resources more efficiently for any purpose including the pursue of our goals and dreams.

This hypnotic lesson will help you give clear instructions and express your desires to your subconscious mind about how you want to feel and treat yourself, **so you can effortlessly achieve your rapid weight loss goals.**

Let's begin now…

Find a nice and cozy place where you won't be disturbed… and before you become completely absorbed with the sound of my voice… make yourself comfortable enough to go **into a state of relaxation... you can sit or lie down...** and close your eyes…

This rapid weight loss mindset begins to activate as soon as you intentionally **start to relax and calm yourself down... just like right now** and by realizing… that when **you fill your mind with relaxing thoughts...** any time of the day… **you will feel more energized, motivated and capable of facing any challenge…**

So as soon as you are ready to **start going into a more relaxed state of mind and body...** simply shift your focus to your breathing. Notice the air going inside your lungs and going out. That's it... now take a deep breath in.... and let it go... gently.... **relaxing... letting go… being at peace…**

And **to continue to deepen your relaxation feeling even more....** take another slow and deep breath in now.... and gently.... let it go... all the way out... **as you feel getting more relaxed**… **going deeper and deeper still into a relaxing and peaceful state of mind**…

And as **you feel getting more relaxed** allow your breathing to naturally happen on its own... collect all the tension when you inhale... and let it all go... **and relax... every time you exhale... deepening your relaxation**… **two times more relaxed** that so far… and don't **relax only like that**… also **deeply relax in any way** that is most natural to you to **relax right now**.... as you listen to my voice and pleasant sounds of this guided hypnosis...

Enjoy that relaxation feeling… and notice where relaxation comes from… notice that place in your body that is most relaxed and think of it as a source of your calmness.... imagining... that from this source, **calming energies are spreading in all directions...** reaching all other parts of your body**...** from head to toes... and from your toes to your head.... **making you have positive and loving thoughts about yourself…** becoming more compassionate to yourself…. kind and gentile in every way… full of understanding and patience for meeting your needs…**

Going into a more compassionate state of mind to naturally start caring more about yourself in a

constructive way... that allows you to be even better to others around you... and feel good about yourself at the end of the day...

Imagine your favorite color coming out of this source of your calming energy and spreading in all directions filling every cell of your body...

Feel how **your favorite color makes you think compassionate and self-loving thoughts...** and notice all muscles in your legs... **getting relaxed**.... your favorite color is filling muscles in your torso.... your chest... your arms and hands... all **filling with this calming energy...** and going deeper into relaxation...

Your entire body is now filled with your favorite color and that calming energy... from head to toes.... and from your toes to your head.... that color is making **you feel have a positive, self-loving and compassionate relationship with yourself... full of understanding and patience for meeting your needs... on your way to successfully accomplishing your rapid weight loss goals...**

At this moment **you are becoming more in tune and completely aligned with your sense of true self... and that connection is getting stronger and stronger...** and as that connection grows stronger, **all positive thoughts and behaviors increase in number to completely support your desire to**

treat yourself with more compassion than ever before...

Your self-care and self-loving thoughts are allowing you to create a strong bond with your true self... and start being more understanding and patient with yourself...

You are feeling so calm and relaxed at this moment... and that allows you to notice and listen to your mind and heart communicating with your true self.... and your true self communicating with your mind and heart...

So far we used our mind for communicating and expressing our desires and needs... and the truth is that you can also **use your heart to communicate with your inner being** your heart is a point of connection where your inner and outer self, come together... a connection between your body and your mind...

Rest your relaxing awareness on your heart... in the center of your chest... and as you concentrate your relaxed awareness on your heart... imagine it expanding like a balloon... growing bigger and bigger... expanding in all directions equally... and feel the compassionate and loving energies from your heart expanding outwards everywhere around you... and imagen you are creating a bubble of compassioned and loving energy beyond your physical body as big as a house... **creating an aura of compassioned and loving heart-energy... feeling completely safe and secure... centered... and deeply relaxed...**

Notice what is your experience at this moment as the **compassioned and loving heart-energy surrounds you... protecting you... keeping you safe and secure... centered and connected to your true self...**

Allow yourself to experience all of the joy and love... a sense of belonging... as you feel the safety that this calming energy radiates from the center of your heart... moving outward… creating an aura big as a house all around you...

Use your heart to clearly communicate and express all your desires and needs... from a place of love.... a place of understanding and patience.... express your intention to **be more compassionate to yourself and to treat yourself with all the love and respect you deserve... so you can effortlessly achieve your rapid weight loss goals...**

Ask your heart to use this calming energy and show you a couple of new all self-loving and self-caring habits in your mind that would create ten times stronger connection with your true self… habits **of caring more about yourself in a constructive way… that will allow you to be even better to others around you… and feel good about yourself at the end of the day…**

It's completely ok if your heart chooses to show you these habits in the form of thoughts or sounds… physical sensations and emotions… or in any other way... open your mind to receive any image, sound or feeling from your heart that would let you know what kind of habits you should start practicing every day so you can become **more compassioned and self-caring about yourself in a constructive way… that will allow you to be even better to others around you… and feel good about yourself at the end of the day…**

With your relaxed attention observe everything that presents itself on your mental screen… and **recognize that one habit that you can start practicing today… and deepen your connection and relationship with your true self… as you progress more easily toward your weight and health goals…**

In a moment, I am going to start counting down from five to one... and when you hear me saying "one" **you will become fully awake, aware and alert… ready**

to start practicing your habit of being more compassionate and self-loving toward yourself...

Five... **slowly starting to come back**... four... becoming aware of the position of your relaxed body... three... becoming aware of space around you... two... **your energy and motivation are growing stronger**... one... open your eyes, stretch your body as you become **fully awake, aware and alert... ready to start practicing your habit of being more compassionate and self-loving toward yourself...**

Evening Routine

(30 minutes)

Hello, and welcome to your Rapid Weight Loss Hypnosis Program For Women, which will help you on your journey by installing the most useful behaviors, motivation, and thinking patterns for rapid weight loss.

This is your nineteenth hypnotic lesson and it will help you to **create a powerful evening routine that you can repeat every day, so you can achieve your ideal weight and health goals much easier.**

In your eighteenth hypnotic lesson, you learned how to become more compassioned and have a more self-loving relationship with yourself. Treating ourselves with understanding, patience, respect and love that we deserve allows us to also create better relationships with others. A loving relationship with yourself and others will surround you with all the necessary support on your way to success.

This hypnotic lesson will suggest the most successful evening routine for that you can use to **peacefully complete your day and develop a habit**

of a healthier lifestyle, that will ultimately lead you to **achieve your weight and health goals**.

Let's begin now…

Find a nice and cozy place where you won't be disturbed… and before you become completely absorbed with the sound of my voice… make yourself comfortable enough to go **into a state of relaxation… you can sit or lie down…** and close your eyes…

This rapid weight loss mindset begins to activate as soon as you intentionally **start to relax and calm yourself down… just like right now** and by realizing… that when **you fill your mind with relaxing thoughts…** any time of the day… **you can set yourself up for good nights rest and rejuvenating sleep…**

Start **instructing your body and mind to relax…** notice how you breathe. And as you start to focus and follow your breathing… I would like you to carefully listen to the sound of my voice that you can hear right now… including the sound of your breathing…

Inhale slowly… hold it for a one second…. and let go… listen to all the sounds you hear including the sound you make as you inhale… and as you exhale… and notice how every time you exhale like this, with your attention resting on the sound of my voice, **you instantly start feeling more relaxed... you start feeling more at ease... allowing yourself to become calm...**

Calmly listen to all the sound, including the sound of your breath, with your awareness and observe mindfully... sounds you make as you inhale... and as you exhale... **feeling so relaxed right now...**

Decide to double your relaxation next time air start going out by exhaling slower than usual... make your exhalation longer... and listen to that sound of exhalation until you **completely let go of all thoughts**.... reminding yourself that this is your time.... and that you are here because **you want to develop an evening routine that will help you calmly complete your day... let go... have a good night's rest to feel refreshed as you continue to work on your rapid weight loss and health goals as soon as you wake up in the morning...**

You can allow yourself to completely clear your mind from all the thoughts, worries and anxieties right now... by becoming aware of your passive awareness... **thoughts are fading away by like mist in the morning... calmly being aware of the inner world... knowing that calm awareness of your inner world can only bring you tranquility and a deep sense of profound relaxation...**

In a moment I am going to start counting from five to one… and when you hear me say "one" **you will completely let go and double your relaxation… and find yourself in a nice and cozy room with a big Tv screen…**

Starting the countdown now… five… **going deeper and deeper into relaxation…** four… **gently letting go and allowing thoughts to pass by**… three… **going deeper and deep into relaxation**… two… **all the way down… all the way down**… one… **completely relax now… deeper and deeper still… double your relaxation… you are in a nice cozy room right now…**

In front of you, in the center of the room, there is a big tv screen… and on the screen, you can see seven tasks that create a powerful evening routine that **you can use to create habits for your rapid weight loss program…**

The first task- Cool down your bedroom

The second task – Drink apple cider vinegar with lemon

The third task – Take a shower

The Fourth task – Check what you accomplished

The fifth task – Winding downtime

The sixth task – Drink herbal tea for calmness

The seventh task - Practice mindfulness and meditation

The movie begins and you watch yourself on that screen doing your powerful evening routine... you see yourself doing each task in a relaxed manner and having fun by doing so...

On the screen you see that moment you when you realize it is time to finish this day and have some well-deserved rest...

On that screen you see yourself doing the first step of your evening routine and that is to **let in some fresh air and make your bedroom slightly colder than usual... this method speeds up your metabolism and burns fat faster than before...** your body is using energy from the fat to keep you warm at night... so don't be surprised when you wake up feeling thinner...

As you let your bedroom get cool down you go to your kitchen and see yourself **having a glass of warm lemon flavored water with apple cider vinegar**... knowing that this task is **helping you detox, improve your immune system and speed up your metabolism so you can start burning fat overnight much quicker...**

After busting your immune system you continue to your third task... you **see yourself taking a shower... you wash away any tension that might**

be accumulated during the day… you wash away all worries and concerns… and you notice how much lighter you feel… completely relaxed…

Watch yourself on that screen going through your to do list and your daily plans… tick all the boxes with completed tasks and realize that you've made progress… you did as much as you could…. Maybe you completed everting maybe there are few left undone… in any case realize that **the best thing to do is to have good night's rest… tell yourself that your day is completed and the only thing you need to do is to fall asleep…**

After deciding to finish thinking for the day **see yourself on that screen doing some winding downtime**… by simply making your lights dimmer… or picking up a nice book to read in your bed… see how winding down twenty to thirty minutes before sleep helps **you have a better night's rest…**

Once you feel that your mind is slowing down… and your breathing becomes even and steady… see yourself having a nice warm cup of herbal tea for calmness… drink your tea to make sure you **go into a deep sleep faster**… so **you can have good quality uninterrupted sleep until morning…**

Once you finish your cup of tea you move on to the next task and that is **your practice of mindfulness**

and meditation… See yourself on that tv screen, **practicing mindful meditation**… doing deep and calm breathwork and… **preparing your mind to go into a wonderful land of dreams…**

The movie continues and you watch yourself **falling a deep restful sleep…** see your body doing all kinds of healing during the night and filing with all necessary energies for the next day… and at the end of the movie **see yourself waking up feeling rejuvenated** and saying to yourself that **this is going to be a great day…**

As the movie comes to an end you imagine that tv screen is becoming smaller and smaller… and once it is small enough, imagine taking that tv screen, that is playing powerful evening routine over and over again and gently place it inside your mind as a symbol of your desire to **have a good night's rest so you can feel refreshed as you continue to work on your rapid weight loss and health goals as soon as you wake up in the morning… do this now and install a powerful evening routine into your inner being…**

In a moment, I am going to start counting down from five to one... and when you hear me saying "one" **you will become fully awake, aware and alert… ready to have a well deserved rest…**

Five... **slowly starting to come back**... four... becoming aware of the position of your relaxed body... three... becoming aware of space around you... two... **your energy and motivation are growing stronger**... one... open your eyes, stretch your body as you become **fully awake, aware and alert... ready to have a well deserved rest...**

Get Enough Sleep

(30 minutes)

Hello, and welcome to your Rapid Weight Loss Hypnosis Program For Women, which will help you on your journey by installing the most useful behaviors, motivation, and thinking patterns for rapid weight loss.

This is your twentieth hypnotic lesson and it will help you to **relax and wind down before you go to deep and restful sleep, so you can achieve your ideal weight and health goals much easier.**

In your nineteenth hypnotic lesson, you learned how to create a perfect evening routine to calmly complete your day and prepare yourself for sleep that supports your weight loss plan. Dedicating purpose to your action will bring you closer to your goals much faster.

This hypnotic lesson will use mindfulness meditation practice to prepare you for better sleep and it is recommended that you listen to this particular recording every time before you go to sleep as a part of your evening routine, **so you can effortlessly achieve your rapid weight loss goals.**

Let's begin now…

Find a nice and cozy place where you won't be disturbed… and before you become completely absorbed with the sound of my voice… make yourself comfortable enough to go **into a state of relaxation… you can sit or lie down…** and close your eyes…

This rapid weight loss mindset begins to activate as soon as you intentionally **start to relax and calm yourself down… just like right now** and by realizing… that when **you fill your mind with relaxing thoughts…** any time of the day… **you will feel more at ease and completely ready to let go…**

Begin your mindfulness practice by taking a few long, slow, deep breaths… inhaling deeply… and exhaling very slowly…. inhale through your nose or mouth and exhale through your nose or mouth… **becoming relaxed**… Feel your belly expand when you breathe in and **relax and let go** as you breathe out…

Become aware of all internal and external sounds… and begin to shift your focus from outside sensations to your internal representation of your inner world… and **sense relaxation starting to fill your body and mind**… focus your attention to your breathing and pleasant sounds of this hypnotic lesson.... and continue to **observe relaxation feelings…**

In a moment I am going to start counting from five to one… and when you hear me say "one" **you will completely let go and double your relaxation…**

Starting the countdown now… five… **going deeper and deeper into relaxation…** four… **gently letting go and allowing thoughts to pass by**… three… **going deeper and deep into relaxation**… two… **all the way down… all the way down**… one… **completely relax now… deeper and deeper still… double your relaxation…**

The best way to prepare yourself for sleep is to **allow any kind of healing to happen overnight**…. Start by imagining a cone of beautiful white light above you... and imagine that cone of beautiful wight light moving down over you... setting upon you healing energy …. everywhere around you... **keeping you safe and secure**… being protected by this white healing light…

You are illuminated by this white healing light… and everything around you seems to be ... more alive… bright... vibrating... sparkling… glowing and moving in rhythmic waves of that white healing light…

Notice all the subtle sensations of this healing energy of the light moving down around your body...

embracing you completely... and as you notice all these subtle sensations imagine this wonderful and pleasant healing light gently entering your head... and makes its way to your neck... traveling down to your shoulders.... white healing light caressing your shoulders....

With your relaxed and passive awareness begin to feel all your muscles soften... relax... let go of any tensions... and completely release any tightness...

Follow the light now and watch it slowly and softly entering your chest... filling the area around your heart... **gently and tenderly comforting your hart and doing any necessary healing... making you feel at peace... fulfilled... and deeply satisfied...**

As you feel deeply satisfied follow the light with your awareness now as it goes down your spine and spreading across all surface of your back and torso...

Entering through your skin and **going deeper and deeper... all the way down... layer after layer... moving deeper and deeper still...** reaching to all your organs... caressing them softly, **cleansing and doing any necessary healing... making you feel at peace... fulfilled... and deeply satisfied...**

The light is now moving toward your stomach... sending waves of healing and calming energy into your belly... softly soothing and warm healing light filling your belly right now... **making you feel completely at ease... safe ad secure...**

This light is now going to visit any part of your body that needs healing... no effort is needed on your side.... Because, this white healing light comes from a divine source of intelligence that is connected to your higher self... and that means this white healing light knows your personal blueprint of your perfect health...

Allow the light to fulfill its healing purpose and visit parts of your body that need any kind of healing...

Observe light moving through your body and immediately finding places where discomfort or anything unpleasant is stored... into any frustration... and **feel those parts of your body open, release and heal** as you watch white healing light revitalize and rejuvenate these parts of your being...

Allow this healing white light softly set upon the middle of your chest and send unlimited healing energy straight into your heart... **removing any blocks or barriers... dissolving any fears and hurt from your paste... giving you a way of preserving perfect health... and automatically getting rid of that which is destructive and damaging...**

And as this happens right now... feel **your body starting to generate only beneficial energies that will completely support your healthy lifestyle...**

While you feel this energy being generated somewhere in your body… and as you begin to see this energy inside your mind's eye... notice white light beginning to merge with this beneficial energy… and see the starting to spiral through your body... moving through and reaching every cell of your body... **filing every cell with strength and perfect health…**

Calmly observe healing happening within you right now... as you are breathing in peace.... and breathing out any nervousness... inhale and fill your lungs... and let go of anything unwonted in your body and mind as you exhale...

And as you breathing in peace, your whole being knows that you are healing right now and continue healing overnight… and every night… so **you can wake up feeling in perfect health and have success in everything you do…**

Once you fall asleep you will begin to breathe deeply in a steady rhythm unconsciously…   and **you will release any negativity overnight... you will breath them out of your body... out of your mind... and make yourself completely free of all worries and concerns…**

While you are at deep sleep **you will release any discomfort or tiredness... breath them out of your**

body... out of your mind... and make yourself completely free of all sadness and fatigue...

With each out breath you release any resentment and hurt... and with each breath in you invite joy and happiness...

At this moment you are feeling at peace and completely calm... and you can allow the light to slowly begin to return to its original source where it came from... **knowing it will watch after you all the time and visit you to do any healing if necessary...**

As the white healing light goes back to the divine source of intelligence you notice light around you becoming softer... everything seems to slow down... it is getting darker... and **you feel completely relaxed... at peace... ready to fall a deep restful rejuvenating sleep...**

Everything is completed for today... **you feel fulfilled... and deeply satisfied... and you can let yourself go and gently drift off into a wonderful land of dreams...**

In a moment, I am going to start counting down from five to one... and when you hear me saying "one" **you will start drifting off into a deep sleep and finally have that well deserved rest at the end of the day...**

Five... **slowly starting to come back**... four... becoming aware of the position of your relaxed body... three... becoming aware of space around you... two... **your energy and motivation are growing stronger**... one... **drifting off into a deep sleep... falling asleep at any moment now... let go... sleep... sleep... sleep**

Put It All Together

(60-90 minutes)

Hello, and welcome to your Rapid Weight Loss Hypnosis Program For Women, which will help you on your journey by installing the most useful behaviors, motivation, and thinking patterns for rapid weight loss.

This is your twenty first hypnotic lesson and it will help you to **put it all together and use everything for this program, so you can achieve your ideal weight and health goals much easier.**

In your twentieth hypnotic lesson, you learned how to prepare yourself with mindfulness meditation to fall a deep restful and rejuvenating sleep. Remember to listen to lesson twenty every night before you go to sleep as a part of your evening routine.

This hypnotic lesson includes all the lessons from this program giving you opportunity to easily remember all steps in your rapid weight loss program, **so you can effortlessly achieve your weight loss and health goals.**

Let's begin now…

Find a nice and cozy place where you won't be disturbed… and before you become completely absorbed with the sound of my voice… make yourself comfortable enough to go **into a state of relaxation... you can sit or lie down…** and close your eyes…

This rapid weight loss mindset begins to activate as soon as you intentionally **start to relax and calm yourself down... just like right now** and by realizing… that when **you fill your mind with relaxing thoughts…** any time of the day… **you will preserve all the learnings and knowledge from this program…**

As you continue to focus on your relaxation... imagine that you are standing at the top of a staircase... and as you look down the staircases you notice that there are 10 steps leading down to a safe room...

In a moment, I'm going to ask you to start going down the steps... and with each step you take, you will become more and more relaxed… I will be counting from ten to one and when you hear me say "one" you will be completely relaxed and find yourself in a safe room…

Start going down the stairs now and step onto step ten... and feel yourself going into relaxation... nine ... going deeper and deeper... eight... relax… seven ... deeper and deeper still... six... feeling so relaxed right now... five... going all the way down deeper and deeper into relaxation ... four ... and deeper still .... three ... feeling very… very relaxed... two ... calmly drifting into a peaceful state of relaxation... one... feeling completely relaxed and in a safe room…

Look around this safe room and find a comfortable place where you can sit or lie down… because it is a movie night and its time to relax…

As you make yourself comfortable a huge movie screen appears in front of you… and the movie is about to start…
Title appears in the middle of the screen… Rapid Weight Loss Hypnosis Program For Women… and you are the leading star…

Now, as **you see yourself standing there with confidence**... think for a moment where that confidence comes from... and most certainly **you will realize that comes from a great sense of purpose.... and from your plans for success, and the way you stick to your SMART action plans....**

See yourself on that screen **confident... with a purpose on your mind... focusing your endless energy toward your big SMART goals** ... where you set your tasks... schedule activities.... milestones... that you are committed to achieving...

Each month has a specific, measurable, attainable, realistic and timed goal... and as you break down your big goal into easily achievable small smart goals.... notice how your confidence is growing by knowing that you will accomplish your weight loss goals and so much more than that...

Having that certainty in your abilities allows you to use your time more efficiently than before... you create plans for success, and you stick to your SMART action plans.... see yourself on that screen **doing what you need to do... set your tasks... schedule activities.... milestones... knowing that you will achieve success...**

Everything you do is SMART.... specific outcomes... measurable results.... achievable monthly goals.... relevant to you... timed perfectly... in order for you to **rapidly start losing weight...**

Think about it now... **you will achieve your weight loss and health goals... you will feel amazing... happy and deeply satisfied...**

Ask yourself... what would all of this give you... what will all of this allow you to have in your life... something that you didn't have but you wanted to have it... you are finally there and you can have it now...

Allow the perfect vision to unfold in front of you right now as you think about all the outcomes and all the benefits that you will receive once you achieved your goals of rapidly losing weight and being in perfect health...

See yourself experiencing and having all the benefits and rewards form having achieved all your big and small rapid weight loss goals...

See who you become as a person... and how much you have grown after this journey...

Notice what do you believe about life and about yourself as you feel that deep satisfaction of having the outcomes that are even better that you expected...

Continue breathing at a steady pace.... just like that... and allow the air moving in and out of your lungs and belly to **deepen your relaxation**...

Imagine that each time you inhale... **relaxation energy washing away all overwhelming expectations... allowing you to effortlessly move toward your rapid weight loss goals... without** pressure... completely at ease... with a strong intention to succeed...

And each new wave of air brings that relaxation energy... fills your head, neck, and chest... just to simply wash away any narrow focus as you exhale.... allowing you to see the big picture... effortlessly let go... release... and free yourself completely from the form of your imagination ... naturally... right now... and allow yourself to be surprised with even better results and even better outcomes... as you give yourself permission to naturally achieve your goals and outcomes in many different forms... with your strong intention...

To make your intention even stronger repeat these affirmations after me inside your mind... and each time you read and repeat any affirmation... imagine that you are saying it louder and louder...

From this moment forward I invite unlimited positivity and motivation into my life!

Repeat it much louder inside your mind...

I am an unlimited and unstoppable source of energy and powerful intention... I can do anything!

Repeat it louder and hear this affirmation echoing into distance everywhere around you…

I am grateful for all the beauty that I have in my life, inside and out!

Turn the volume up… let your voice reach all corners of the Earth…

In every challenge I see the opportunity to grow and achieve my goals!

Repeated even louder than before…

One more affirmation…

I attract the best circumstances and people in my life with my positive mindset… I have everything I need to achieve my rapid weight loss goals!

Repeat it in your mind so loudly that the whole universe can hear you…

As soon as you repeat these affirmations **notice how much more energy and motivation you have…**

Focus this power on creating a calendar for the whole year… make all the entries and schedule all activities, actions and habits for each day of the year… that you are going to take in order to **achieve your rapid weight loss goals… making sure that they fit your healthy lifestyle…**

Every time you see the reminder to do some activity, take action or install a habit you will **feel great will power and your desire to be consistent** because you know it will pay off and you will achieve success…

Choose an assistant you like that will be perfect for this function and suitable for your personal needs… someone who knows how to remind you in the right moment so you **instantly start feeling increased will power and desire to be consistent with your healthy life choices…**

Now a**lign your consistency in taking action with playfulness… find a perfect balance between being working and being playful**… and realize you can have the best of both of these worlds…

Recognize that inner child inside you and **reconnect with all the fun and joy that you can experience while pursuing your rapid weight loss goals…**

That inner child is always present inside you and waiting for your permission to **start playing and fully express that inherited trait to enjoy life and**

enjoy the journey… as you rapidly lose weight as you have fun…

Imagine that everything you do, you are either **being completely playful, or you have that perfectly balanced playful personality that allows you to be serious enough and have fun at the same time**… imagine now what this would be like…

See yourself… **being completely playful as you are doing some activities on your own… and see yourself playfully get the job done…**

And all of this is happening because you wake up and start your day with right frame of mind and with a powerful morning routine…
On the screen you see that the moment you wake up you stretch, and you think to yourself that **this is going to be a great day…**

You get out of the bed and once you are ready you go to your kitchen and **have a glass or two of warm lemon flavored water**… **detox, improve your immune system and speed up your metabolism so you can start losing weight much quicker…**

You go **out for fresh air, to catch some sun and go for a power walk… knowing that this task will increase your energies and burn fat faster than before…**

See yourself taking a cold shower… you wash away any remaining negativity… and improved circulation boosts your immune system and makes you become more focused and alert…

Enjoying a high-protein breakfast… that regulates your appetite, feeds your muscles and burns more calories…

Practice mindfulness and meditation… See yourself on that screen, **practicing mindful meditation**…setting your intentions for that day… starting with the first step of preparing your diet for the whole day…

And move to deciding how are you going to feel during your day… **what positive emotions are you going to experience**… how will you behave and react to different situations… how will you meet any challenges if they occur…

See yourself on that screen setting clear intentions for that day and **accomplishing everything you wanted to do that day… feeling deeply satisfied at the end of the perfect day…**

Be completely still and mindful… Noticing how the mind is trying to invite you to get involved in the content of the thoughts and create a story… **stay calm and keep observing without wanting to change anything** or to interact with any of your thoughts… **let them go… you are only a witness of**

your thoughts that are passing by just like clouds in the sky… coming and going… thoughts fading away…

Whatever emotion appears inside your body or mind welcome it… become aware of it **without a desire to act upon it… just let it be there…** present together with you at this moment…

Remember to be completely still and mindful… stay calm and keep observing without wanting to change anything or to interact with any of your emotions… positive or negative… **let them go… you are only a witness of your present emotions** that are passing by just like clouds in the sky… coming and going…

Use mindfulness to develop greater self-control… try to take one piece of your favorite food and bring it closer to your face… smell and mindfully become aware of all sensations and everything else going on inside your body and mind…

Gently place that piece of food into your mouth…. And let it rest there for a second or two without chewing or swallowing it… allow it to be there as you notice the flavor and texture… and above all… **notice your self-control…**

Bring your focus back to your breath that is going from the top of your head down to the bottom of your toes… **and notice how your awareness of this present moment, your self-control, and your satisfaction becomes even stronger as you mindfully choose and decide to eat small amounts of delicious, nutritious and low calorie food…**

Enjoy being in this safe and secure place as you are listening to this hypnotic lesson and **fill your mind and body with only positive intentions… that will allow you to achieve your weight and health goals faster than before…**

Give yourself permission to enjoy positivity that comes with this place… and notice how easy it is for you to objectively feel and experience all emotions when you feel calmness… notice how it easy for you to recognize emotions that are stimulating self-sabotaging behaviors… and notice **how easy it becomes for you to interrupt those emotions with your strong intention and willpower to stop self-sabotage…**

In fact, whenever you notice any emotion that encourages any kind of self-sabotage you will think of your safe and secure place, **intensify feelings of determination to rapidly lose weight that you are feeling now…. And immediately stop self-sabotage of any kind… including stopping self-sabotage eating…**

Enjoy this amazing safe place now **and relax even more than before... as you feel your intention and willpower to stop self-sabotage eating become stronger... and find yourself rapidly losing weight...**

From now on, if it happens you feel any kind of craving, your remember your protective and healing **color... and it will immediately locate the part of your body with craving sensations... and remove that feeling and restore your mind and body to perfect calmness... filling you with peace, health and happiness... that allows you to effortlessly pursue your weight loss and health goals...**

Sometimes it will happen so fast you would be able to notice it, and other times you will **consciously use your color to remove any cravings...**

Your mental gastric band to reduce cravings is now completely installed... and you might find yourself being surprised how much more choice you have now to **reduce cravings and stick to your diet plan...**

If it happens by any chance that you ever begin to feel anxious, worried, concerned, or stressful, for whatever reason, start thinking about water... any kind of water... and you'll **immediately wash away all your anxieties, worries, concerns and stress... become completely relax... and that will allow** your mind and body to function more effectively … so you can spontaneously and effortlessly lose weight rapidly….

When you are relaxed everything works better… your mindset is better… you feel more energy inside your body… and your body uses that energy to functions better… your body uses this relaxed energy to **improve your health in many ways… including speeding up your metabolism to burn fat more easily…**

At this moment **you are deciding to start drinking more water** on a regular basis… and **the more water you drink, the better you feel…**

Every glass of water you drink makes you feel relaxed… because water can collect all negativity, all worries and simply wash them away…

All these good decisions create the future of your dreams…

Let's have a look at what your mind would predict now when **you make the right decision and choose to eat healthy food and exercise…**

Imagine now that **you're doing what you know is good for you**…. in your everyday life there is only space for healthy food and plenty of physical activities including exercising…

See yourself doing this day after day, week after week and month after month… eating only healthy food and being super active…

Now jump forward two – three - four years into the future… **experience joy, happiness and fulfillment… knowing that even better future awaits you in ten years from now… feel all the benefits of your success…**

As you experience these benefits, **you know that you made the right choice**… and all of these amazing things are happening to you just because you made that one small step today…. **toward the right decision…**

This beautiful and bright future ahead of you totally pushes away that other unpleasant future… **making you completely forget about all the junk food…**

This logical prediction of your mind allows you to **be smart with every choice you make**, and in time **it gets easier and easier for you to make the right choices… because It's easy to make choices that are beneficial for you today and tomorrow…**

Starting today, follow your good choice **and find yourself doing whatever is necessary to achieve your rapid weight loss goals and perfect health…**

Make your intention stronger by installing these powerful beliefs… repeat them inside your mind after me… and each time you read and repeat any belief… imagine that you are saying it louder and louder…

I am happily achieving my rapid weight loss goals!

Repeat it much louder inside your mind…

I now clearly see myself at my ideal weight in perfect health!

Repeat it louder and hear this belief echoing into distance everywhere around you…

I deserve to have a slim, healthy and attractive body!

Turn the volume up… let your voice reach all corners of the Earth…

I celebrate my own power to make choices around food!

Repeated even louder than before…

One more powerful belief…

I am the creator of my future and the driver of my mind! I will succeed!

Repeat it in your mind so loudly that the whole universe can hear you…

As soon as you repeat these empowering beliefs **notice how much more confidence, motivation and certainty you have…**

Allow yourself for these powerful seeds to grow even bigger and stronger… and create an unstoppable belief system that will lead you to your desired destination…

Feel the gratitude that comes with this strong belief system…

Gratitude is the key emotion to establishing better rapport with your subconscious mind and to create that mutual trust between your consciousness and your subconsciousness…

This gratitude will connect all your desires with your capabilities to successfully accomplish your rapid weight loss goals…

Express your gratitude to your hair for being there to protect your scalp and make you look beautiful…

Feel the gratitude for your skeleton as it gives you support and protection… to **move easily toward your weight loss and health goals…**

Start feeling grateful for all the intelligence you have… think about all the amazing functions of your brain and what your brain is making you be capable of… and as you do that **express your deep gratitude for having a brain and mind that is dedicated to achieving your weight loss goals…**

Focus on your eyes… and **be thankful for the sense of sight**… and your **ability to see all the benefits of your new healthier lifestyle…**

Now pay attention to your nose… **and thank your nose for the ability to have a sense of smell** which allows you to enjoy the most pleasant aromas… give thanks to this and other abilities of your nose…. **including the ability to smell good opportunities and success ahead of you…**

Think about the perfection of your mouth and tongue… **and thank your mouth for the sense of taste** which allows you to enjoy many different flavors… and **give thanks to your tongue for your ability to speak….**

Allow your consciousness to move toward your throat and your stomach… **express your gratitude** toward your stomach for its digestive capability…

ability to extract all the vitamins and minerals from the food that is necessary for your health …

Think of all the organs in your stomach area… think about your liver, pancreas, spleen, gallbladder, small intestine, large intestine… think about all the amazing functions they do… and **thank these organs for the important role they play in everyday weight loss functions of your body....**

Think about your kidneys end **feel the gratitude for their function of cleaning your blood of toxins** and wastes from your bloodstream...

Thank your blood veins and arteries for providing circulation of the blood to all parts of your body and feeding your entire body with a powerful imine system...

Now take a deep breath in… and as you shift your focus to your breathing think about your lungs... and **express your gratitude for providing oxygen to your body...**

Visit your heart… **feel deep gratitude for your heart** and it continues beating and pumping blood to all parts of your body non-stop...

And finally think about the skin that covers your body... and **express your gratitude for all the functions of your skin…**

The subconscious mind is completely in charge of your body... the way it develops... the way your body moves... and your conscious mind is in charge of your subconscious mind... and that means **you can tell your subconscious mind how to use your body... you can use your mind to improve your body just the way you want it...**

Knowing this, **use your creativity and imagination to create an image of a healthy active body**... start now, and **imagine a healthy body filled with energy and capable of doing all the activities you deep enjoy and you deeply desire... imagine all these fun activities naturally burning fat... losing extra weight... building your body stronger... capable of doing anything your heart desires...**

You are in perfect health... You are filled with active energy... You love your everyday physical activities... Every day in every way you are becoming more and more active...

Your subconscious mind loves to follow your instructions and is working around the clock to **make this happen for you**... giving you all the necessary support... generating and **creating endless amounts of energy... positivity and good vibrations so you can achieve your rapid weight**

loss goals effortlessly... faster than you ever imagined...

Now, rest your relaxing awareness on your heart... in the center of your chest... and as you concentrate your relaxed awareness on your heart... imagine it expanding like a balloon... growing bigger and bigger... expanding in all directions equally... and feel the compassionate and loving energies from your heart expanding outwards everywhere around you... and imagen you are creating a bubble of compassioned and loving energy beyond your physical body as big as a house... **creating an aura of compassioned and loving heart-energy... feeling completely safe and secure... centered... and deeply relaxed...**

Notice what is your experience at this moment as the **compassioned and loving heart-energy surrounds you... protecting you... keeping you safe and secure... centered and connected to your true self...**

Allow yourself to experience all of the joy and love... a sense of belonging... as you feel the safety that this calming energy radiates from the center of your heart... moving outward… creating an aura big as a house all around you... **and deepen your connection and relationship with your true self...**

as you progress more easily toward your weight and health goals…

Watch the screen now and see that moment you when you realize it is time to finish this day and have some well-deserved rest…

On that screen you see yourself doing the first step of your evening routine and that is to **let in some fresh air and make your bedroom slightly colder than usual… this method speeds up your metabolism and burns fat faster than before…**

Next, you go to your kitchen and see yourself **having a glass of warm lemon flavored water with apple cider vinegar**… knowing that this task is **helping you detox, improve your immune system and speed up your metabolism so you can start burning fat overnight much quicker…**

See yourself taking a shower… you wash away any tension that might be accumulated during the day… you wash away all worries and concerns… and you notice how much lighter you feel… completely relaxed…

Watch yourself on that screen going through your to do list and your daily plans… tick all the boxes with completed tasks and realize that you've made progress… you did as much as you could…. Maybe you completed everting maybe there are few left undone… in any case realize that **the best thing to do is to have good night's rest… tell yourself that your day is completed and the only thing you need to do is to fall asleep…**

After deciding to finish thinking for the day **see yourself on that screen doing some winding downtime**… by simply making your lights dimmer… or picking up a nice book to read in your bed… see how winding down twenty to thirty minutes before sleep helps **you have a better night's rest…**

Once you feel that your mind is slowing down… and your breathing becomes even and steady… see yourself having a nice warm cup of herbal tea for calmness… drink your tea to make sure you **go into a deep sleep faster**… so **you can have good quality uninterrupted sleep until morning…**

Once you finish your cup of tea you move on to the next task and that is **your practice of mindfulness and meditation…** See yourself on that tv screen, **practicing mindful meditation**… doing deep and calm breathwork and… **preparing your mind to go into a wonderful land of dreams…**

And the best way to prepare yourself for sleep is to **allow any kind of healing to happen overnight**…. Start by imagining a cone of beautiful white light above you... and imagine that cone of beautiful wight light moving down over you... setting upon you healing energy .... everywhere around you... **keeping you safe and secure**… being protected by this white healing light…

With your relaxed and passive awareness begin to feel all your muscles soften... relax... let go of any tensions... and completely release any tightness...

Entering through your skin and **going deeper and deeper... all the way down... layer after layer... moving deeper and deeper still...** reaching to all your organs... caressing them softly, **cleansing and doing any necessary healing... making you feel at peace... fulfilled... and deeply satisfied...**

Allow the light to fulfill its healing purpose and visit parts of your body that need any kind of healing...

Observe light moving through your body and immediately finding places where discomfort or anything unpleasant is stored... into any frustration... and **feel those parts of your body open, release and heal** as you watch white healing light revitalize and rejuvenate these parts of your being...

And as this happens right now… feel **your body starting to generate only beneficial energies that will completely support your healthy lifestyle...**

In a moment, I am going to start counting down from five to one... and when you hear me saying "one" **you will become fully awake, aware and alert... ready to put it all together and use everything for this program so you can effortlessly achieve your weight loss and health goals...**

Five... **slowly starting to come back**... four... becoming aware of the position of your relaxed body... three... becoming aware of space around you... two... **your energy and motivation are growing stronger**... one... open your eyes, stretch your body as you become **fully awake, aware and alert... put it all together and use everything for this program so you can effortlessly achieve your weight loss and health goals.**